D1536315

Want to be a REAL Man?

Choosing the Good Life!

Dennis G. Aaberg

xulon PRESS

Want to be a REAL Man?
Choosing the Good Life!
by *Dennis G. Aaberg*

Printed in the United States of America

ISBN 9781622304554

Inspiration from the Holy Spirit.

Webster's Third New International Dictionary. (1986). Springfield, Massachusetts: MERRIAM-WEBSTER, INC., Publishers.

www.xulonpress.com

Preface

Recognizing that many, if not most, of the world's problems are caused by men behaving badly through pride, arrogance, or ignorance, this book purposes to provide guidance to mature men into the joyful, content, prosperous REAL men God intends them to be – increasing their benefit to their family, themselves, society, and the world.

Human pride is the basic root of nearly all suffering in the world. Because of that, I spend considerable time dealing with the issue of pride – what it looks like and its devastating effects on relationships and societies. In contrast, I reveal how humility brings healing, honor, success, and favor with God and man. A humble walk with God and man leads to inner peace, contentment, and prosperity of every kind – spiritual, physical, emotional, and financial.

I write this book from a Christian perspective and accept the Bible as the revealed truth, nature, and plan of God. I know through my lifelong experience growing in relationship to my Lord and Savior *Christ Jesus* that He *is the way, the truth, and the life* – the only way through which we will reach heaven and experience the abundant life on this earth that He promises to all who believe in Him and obey Him. A life without Christ is one constantly seeking happiness but never finding it for more than a fleeting moment. The world offers many attractive substitutes, but substitutes never bring the lasting satisfaction they promise.

The inner peace that is beyond human understanding is available only through Christ Jesus, and you will only experience it after accepting Him as your Lord and Savior and receiving the gift of His Holy Spirit to increase your wisdom, understanding, and abundance in every area of your life. You will find as you seek to mature your relationship with God – Father, Son, and Holy Spirit – He will increasingly bless you to enhance your joy, and you can bless others.

I believe you will benefit from my experiences and what God has taught me thus far in my life to enable you to increasingly enjoy an abundant life with a minimum of pain and disappointment. We all experience our own disappointments and pains in life, but I purpose through this book to help you avoid as many as possible and provide you with the needed information to increase your spiritual, emotional, physical, relational, and financial health.

Table of Contents

Chapter 1

A snap-shot of my life

Introduction

*B*y sharing a brief snapshot of my life story, I purpose to give you a sense of how family, friends, schoolmates, and others influence our life's direction as we grow into adulthood and how many of those influences can prevent us from becoming the REAL men God wills us to become – successful leaders in the body of Christ, our families, our communities, and the world in which we live.

Because of the love and attachments we develop with parents, relatives, and friends, most of us grow up accepting what they say as truth, and we tend to follow their examples and advice, turning into creatures of habit based on their training and opinions. But we are all flawed. Our parents, relatives, other adults, and peers in our lives weren't always and aren't always correct in their thinking, opinions, or actions. If we simply copy their behavior and blindly accept everything they say, we may pass on bad teachings and unhealthy habits to our own children without even realizing it and rob ourselves of the good life God wills for us.

God clearly tells us to honor (respect) our parents and elders, but that doesn't mean we should blindly believe everything they tell us. As with everything we hear, see, or read, we should question it in our own minds and hearts, and test it against the Word of God as revealed in the Holy Bible to see if their words and advice are consistent with God's will, nature, and plan, especially if we feel in our heart and spirit that we are being misled.

With that in mind, I now share a brief overview of my life to help you think and process through your own life story to see if you are where you should be in life according to God's plan for you, or if you are blindly following a path others have steered you down.

Christian background

I was fortunate to grow up in a God-fearing family. My parents took me to church and taught me to trust in Jesus. My relatives on both my mother's and father's sides of the family also were, for the most part, devoted Christians.

That said, we also had a buffet of Christian denominations represented within the family, and they all had slightly different twists on how to live your life for Christ and what it meant to be a Christian. Since our beliefs define us and determine how we approach life, this sometimes created confusion as I grew.

My father's influence

My mother and father both grew up on farms in Minnesota during the Great Depression years and World War II and, as was quite common in those days, only received schooling through the eighth grade. My father and mother moved off the farm before I was born to make a life in a rural Minnesota town. My father worked at the local fish hatchery, a small gas station, and finally, as a mechanic at the local Chevy dealer when I was young.

My father was employed as a car mechanic until I was in early elementary school; then he began taking a correspondence course in radio and television repair. During that education process, he set up a television and radio repair shop in the basement of our home when I was seven or eight years old. He began repairing radios and televisions for neighbors at night and worked as a mechanic during the day. He worked long hours to provide for us – a growing family of five children, me being the oldest.

As his television and radio repair work load increased, my father could no longer keep up with the repair work at night on a part-time basis, so, when I was thirteen years old, he took a big step by quitting his mechanic job and renting a small building in a neighboring small town to pursue his own business full-time. Since he couldn't afford to hire any help at that time, I started working for him and have been working steady ever since.

There were many times I didn't appreciate having to work at that age. I wanted to be out playing all summer long and after school with my friends, but Dad needed help, and I was his best option at the time. Reflecting on that experience now, I really appreciate the time I was able to spend with my dad working and the experience I gained working in his store and interacting with the public on a daily basis. God's Word teaches that *"all things work together for good to those who love God and are called according to His purpose,"* and I know that is true partially because I can see now how that experience, working for my dad, has benefited me throughout my life.

Through the passage of time – much of it spent with my father – I gained an inaccurate view of who I am. As I said earlier, we are "all" flawed, and my dad was no exception.

Many of the businessmen in the community had graduated from high school and many had a college degree. I remember my dad referring to a number of other successful educated men in various careers as "big shots," so through that I began to develop an image of myself as being inferior to other people in certain walks of life. I began to see myself as a lower-class person who was restricted in what I could achieve or be in life. I began to form the idea that college and higher education were for others – those smarter than I. So I began to order my life according to the expectations I embraced from my father's speech and attitude, developing low expectations for what I could accomplish or be in life. My father also taught me honesty, integrity, hard work, and commitment, and those are invaluable Godly characteristics for any REAL man to live by.

My father was successful. He was a good father, provider, and business man. I now realize, however, that my father tended to think small concerning himself and his abilities. As his son, I have tended to emulate that limited thinking concerning my own abilities and possibilities for success in my life.

On the spiritual side, I remember my father being a faithful usher at the church we attended, and he helped with the service radio broadcasts later in his life. My parents' faith in God and taking us to church every Sunday had an overwhelming influence on my life.

The importance of a father's influence

I have loved God and sought to walk in His ways since early childhood, but I have found myself frequently feeling like I disappoint Him. Through most of my adult life I have felt like the things I enjoy doing and the ministry work I engage are somehow not important enough to please God. I have struggled to shed the feeling that I must to be doing something "more important." As I have prayed and struggled to understand this and God's will for my life, I am finally seeing with more clarity why I have felt this way.

While I was growing up, it seemed all that was important to my dad was work, while all that was important to me was being free to enjoy outdoor activities and play sports with my friends. My dad considered sports a waste of time. I recall several occasions when he voiced that opinion in my company. And when he said it, I could hear tones of resentment in his voice. I never discovered why he felt that way, and he has since passed away so I will never know the source of his feelings about sports now. But I loved sports so much that I kept playing anyway – every chance I could.

My dad never once saw a game I played all the way through high school. After I was discharged from the United Sates Army and was playing town team baseball, I remember one Sunday afternoon seeing my mom and dad drive up to the field. I could hardly believe it, but they only stayed a short time before driving off.

I know my dad loved me. He tried showing it by doing things for me and giving me things that were important to him. For instance, he bought for me my first three cars during the years I worked for him. I believe to a large extent he did that because cars were important to him. In all honesty, I may have found nearly as much joy in receiving a high quality baseball glove or pair of baseball shoes from him, or seeing him attend my baseball games. This is the big mistake many of us make. We do for others what we would like done for us instead of what they want done for them. We have perverted the Golden

Rule. The Lord Jesus said to *"Do unto others what you would have them do unto you"* to demonstrate your love. That means we seek to discover what is important to others and do that for them. *Loving others means you do for them what is important to them – not necessarily to you.*

Don't misunderstand me. I very much appreciated and enjoyed the cars, but if cars had not been so important to my dad, he likely would not have bought them for me. Now I understand that was my father's way of demonstrating his love for me. I wish now I had realized that as a young man. If I had, I would have been more thankful and appreciative than I was.

A mistake I believe many fathers make is simply following the pattern of their fathers when it comes to raising children. I have heard many fathers say, *"It was good enough for me, so it is good enough for my kids."* It is almost as if fathers are trying to win their father's approval by training their sons in the ways of their fathers. Depending on the fatherly example, this could be tragic. That is why it is vitally important to train our sons and daughters in the ways of God as found in the Holy Bible. Our heavenly Father provides for us in His recorded Testimony wisdom, understanding, and guidance to live successful lives and properly train our children. Our earthly fathers may or may not have passed on that perfect training to us.

As I learned more of my dad's family history, I think he may have struggled with many of the same self-esteem and acceptance issues that I have struggled with, and he inadvertently transferred those issues to me. My grandfather was an immigrant farmer from Norway who traveled by ship to the United States as a young man to make a life in America. From what I have been told by some of his peers, he was a tough, strong, and hard working man. Considering the challenging life my grandfather likely encountered as a farmer during the turn of the twentieth century, I believe he felt a duty as a father to make his son tough and teach him to work hard. It sounded as though my dad didn't receive many pats on the back for work well done – things were just expected. Upon reflection, I think my dad struggled with feeling accepted and loved by his father as I have learned that I likely have.

Current revelations

It has helped me recently to understand the probable source of my tendency to feel I am disappointing God. Father's heavily influence their children's lives. In my opinion, that is why we have so many problems in our world today—there seem to be far too few mature Godly father examples and role models in our modern world, certainly too few Godly role models in general. If you want to see the world change into a better place and see your children grow up healthy, strong, content, and prosperous, the place to start is with you. Our children watch us, fathers, and they tend to emulate our behaviors and believe what we teach them more so than anyone else. We – you – are vitally important!

Therefore, I urge you to develop a relationship with your Lord and Savior, Christ Jesus, so you can discover your true self. It is only when you walk the path prepared for you by God that you will find lasting inner joy, peace, and contentment. If you model your life based on the opinions of others, you will likely live in a constant state of confusion and disappointment because others will likely have varied opinions about how you should live your life based on their own narrow-minded and often misguided picture.

I have come to realize that in subconsciously feeling like I disappointed my father by not sharing all the same values, I have projected that image onto my heavenly Father. I have struggled to shed the feeling that I must to be doing the work others consider more important if I want to please God. This, of course, is absurd! We are all unique children of God with differing likes, dislikes, talents, abilities, and dreams. Each of us pleases God when we trust Him, enjoy with thankfulness and gratitude what He provides for us, and use our money, talents, and abilities to bless the lives of others. He only looks at what we do with the talents, abilities, and resources He has blessed us with. God never compares us to anyone else.

Another reason for feeling unworthy is one I would rather not consider but must. It is possible that through pride I have wanted to do something highly visible and recognizable by the masses so I can feel like I am worthy of God's acceptance. But then I am no longer depending on God's mercy and grace, I am depending on my own God-given abilities, talents, and goodness to solicit God's approval, which will never happen. Too many Christians fall into this trap of feeling like they are acceptable to God and will go to Heaven through their self-judged goodness compared to their internal standard or current worldly standards. This will never happen. The only way to Heaven is through the sacrificial Blood of Jesus the Christ. God will never view any of us acceptable or pleasing through any other means.

My mother's influence

Mom is a baby-sitter and has been since her youth. As I write this, she is soon 88 years old and baby-sitting four great-grandchildren on nearly a daily basis – all under the age of seven. Since her earliest youth, she has always had small children under foot.

Mother loves her family and her relatives – they are her life. She knows the date of every birthday and anniversary of our family and extended families. She is a walking encyclopedia of family dates and history. For her, getting and sending cards to recognize birthdays, anniversaries, and other events is very important. And she looks forward every day to the possibility of getting letters from loved ones so she can keep up on their lives.

I learned to take my cares to Jesus from my mom. What I remember most about Mom as I was growing up is when I went to her for advice or with a problem, she seemed to be always pointing me to Jesus. She emphasized repeatedly that Jesus loved me and would take care of me, so not to worry. That belief and knowledge was etched in my mind and heart as a child – Jesus loves me! Through the many negative circumstances experienced throughout my life, however, that knowledge had trouble staying in my heart. My head was still convinced, but my heart sometimes struggled to believe God really loved me at times when emotional struggles came.

Maybe you have experienced the same difficulties. If God loves you, why do so many negative things happen? How do you trust a God who lets bad things happen to you? I have learned that God is faithful, and He is always there helping us through each struggle and temptation. As we declare a belief in God, Satan comes against us by manipulating negative circumstances to test our faith to see if we really believe in our heart what we say we believe with our mouth. Sometimes, that test gets mighty strong. So I encourage you to believe in your heart and remain strong. God is there protecting and providing for you every moment of every day. Stand strong and resist Satan's attempts to deceive you into doubting God, and you will find your peace return and Satan flee. Just as with Jesus, however, Satan will return at an opportune time when you are weak for one reason or another to test you again. But be assured, God is not too weak to help you; nor has He forsaken you in those moments.

Mom generally seemed to have good advice. Her predominant message was to trust Jesus, stay clear of negative influences, and always strive to do the right thing. Consequently, I learned to walk my own path when necessary; even when it meant walking away from friends or changing friends.

Mom was always encouraging; which I think most mothers tend to be. Whenever I felt inadequate in any way, I would moan about it to Mom, and she would encourage me in the Lord. I usually left mom's presence convinced, for the moment at least, that I was okay. I think my mother overlooks her children's' and family's flaws to a fault, but perhaps that is the way God designed mothers. At any rate, I always went away from Mom feeling better about myself and with more courage to face the next battle.

The influence of childhood classmates

School was mostly an unpleasant experience for me. Partially due to the insecurity I embraced due to the influence of my father's insecurities, I felt inferior to many of the other students who acted more confidently than I – those I viewed as being smarter and superior to me because of their family's social status or because of their school involvement. For example, I came to see class officers, those leading academic or extra-curricular groups, and those taking what I considered difficult classes as being superior to me. I tended to mentally categorize them as "big shots" and myself as stupid in comparison to them. When one of them would make fun of me or degrade me in some way, I took that as confirmation that I really was inferior and stupid. So I came to hate school and just wanted to graduate and get out! That coupled with the fact that for my personality, I just wanted to be outside playing and enjoying physical activity and nature I felt like I was in prison. Recently I learned that I likely am saddled with Attention Deficit Disorder, too, so that almost certainly contributed to my trouble concentrating in school and influencing my low self-esteem.

I can still hear the words and see the face of one particular classmate who ridiculed me when I was doing my best. The first instance was in second or third grade. Everyone in class took turns bringing a treat to school. When it was my turn, my mother sent me to school with a bag of cookies. When cookie-time approached, I counted my classmates and then counted the cookies and discovered there weren't enough cookies for everyone. My solution was to break the cookies in two halves to share so everyone would get at least half a cookie. Well, the kid I mentioned laughed at me and called me cheap or some such thing, and then everyone else started laughing at me. I again took that as confirmation of my stupidity and the inferiority of my family.

Then one day in tenth grade as our basketball team ran drills in practice, I goofed up and ran the wrong route. The same kid that degraded me earlier threw the basketball into my face and called me stupid. That physically and emotionally painful moment again confirmed my feelings of inferiority. As you might expect, he was the son of a successful businessman in town and a class officer.

Those two instances, along with the already low self-esteem, caused me to think for much of my life that I was born to be a lower class individual, lacking the ability to achieve anything of importance. Other than those two instances that are etched in my mind, I have no recollection of any other specific instances of anyone degrading me at school. If they did, I do not remember them. I remember feeling inferior to anyone "popular" because they all seemed to display the high self-confidence that I sorely lacked. Perhaps I envied them or resented them simply because they possessed the self-confidence I lacked and wanted. My classmates probably had nothing but good thoughts toward me, but in my mind I imagined all the popular kids thinking I was stupid. What a waste of precious time – worrying about what people think.

From that, I want you to realize the tendency we can have to believe the worst about ourselves. Throughout my life, I have received encouragement, honors, and recognition in many forms. Because of the feelings of inferiority I embraced as a youngster, however, I have often found ways to explain compliments and honors away, convincing myself that I didn't do anything special – anyone could have done it. I found ways of comparing my accomplishments and recognitions to those of others that I felt had more prominent accomplishments, thereby diminishing mine to nothingness.

I have come to realize that this is essentially a pride issue. When we feel snubbed by others or find ourselves comparing ourselves to others, we are in a state of pride. This is the essence of the anti-God state of mind. We find God telling us frequently in the Holy Bible that He resists the proud and brings down the arrogant while He exalts and lifts up the humble. If we are walking humbly with God, we will experience a calm confidence knowing that God is our protector, provider, and comforter. In a state of humility, we won't be comparing ourselves to others or be trying to achieve self-imagined importance (arrogance). Humility brings the realization that we are important to God and He loves us.

We are unique sons created in His image for a specific purpose. We are not like anyone else, and we shouldn't compare our achievements to those of anyone else. God doesn't compare you to others, and neither should you. He judges you based on the fruit you produce with what He has given you.

The opposite side of our coin containing the inferiority face contains the superiority face. This side elevates your self-esteem (pride) to where you come to think of yourself as the center of the universe. Those suffering from too high a self-esteem tend to have little consideration for the feelings or physical needs of others. You come to be so self-centered that you use people to your advantage and believe it is your right to always receive and not give. This state is obviously more personally destructive than the inferiority side of the coin because God resists the proud, as we will learn in Chapter 2.

Through pride, we inflict harm on others to elevate our self imagined importance. By doing so, we harm ourselves through fractured relationships, and we forfeit God's blessings of peace, joy, and contentment. Only the humble experience the peace and joy of God and contentment in every circumstance. As God's Testimony reveals over and over again, *"God resists the proud but give grace to the humble."* Do you want to experience a life filled with joy, inner peace, contentment, and physical, spiritual, emotional, and financial prosperity? Then humble yourself under God's mighty hand and watch him work miracles in your life.

You will find overcoming pride and walking humbly with God a central theme of this book because that is where prosperity and contentment are realized – in a humble walk with God.

The early years through high school

God's first direct intervention in my life that I recall was the summer following my third grade year in school. It was the first day of little league baseball practice and I was sitting at the top of the hill behind the school watching the boys warm up on the baseball field below. I remember sitting there afraid to go down because some of the "big shot" kids were down there, as well as a couple neighborhood bullies who seemed to like picking on me. I felt extremely intimidated as I sat there alone. Then, I know by divine appointment, the baseball coach came out of the school from behind me and walked past me as I sat on the curb with baseball glove in hand. He asked me if I wanted to play baseball, and I said "Yes." He said, "Come on." Suddenly, I felt a great deal of confidence as we walked down the hill with his hand on my shoulder. I felt protected and safe. He was a patient and loving coach who taught us great fundamentals in baseball that I have since been able to pass on to my own sons and others that I have coached in baseball and softball over the years.

My first trophy was a first place trophy for our team winning the baseball little league tournament championship game when I was in sixth grade. After the game, we, as the winning team, were each rewarded with a used baseball out of the baseball bag as our trophy (a little different than what kids get today) and it was a great thrill. I am now sixty years old and I still have that baseball sitting on my trophy shelf with the date and final score written on it, along with my win-loss record as a pitcher for that season.

Baseball, and subsequently softball, became a big part of my life. God blessed me with athletic ability that has allowed me to enjoy a variety of sports for most of my life and play on a state and national championship softball team. God has blessed me with the coaching ability to lead little league teams to win championship games and opportunities to be a Godly influence in their lives. All of those blessings and opportunities began with a divine hook-up on that summer morning when the Lord brought the baseball coach by to ask me if I wanted to play baseball. I know I would never have had the confidence to walk down that hill if he hadn't come by.

If you are seeking God, He will bring opportunities and blessings into your life. Many times, He brings them through other people, and oftentimes, through unexpected ways. Therefore, you must keep your spiritual ears and eyes open to recognize them when they appear. Many times, you must make a choice to accept or reject the invitation or blessing. It is important that you know God wants you to be happy and enjoy success, but He won't generally pull or push you through a door He opens for you – He lets you choose. As I sat on that hill watching the baseball team warm up, I could have rejected the invitation to play baseball because of the fear and intimidation I was feeling. If I had, I don't know how that would have changed my life, but it likely would have steered me down an entirely different path. Nearly every choice we make in life has eternal consequences.

Throughout high school, I was an above average baseball pitcher, but that only slightly boosted my confidence. Baseball was, however, one of the few things I felt I had some talent for, so that may be partially why I loved it so much. With thoughts of my inferiority etched in my mind, I seemed to focus on my failures and imperfections rather than my successes, however. For instance, I could strike out twelve batters in a game and feel like a failure if I gave up one hit or a walk. It seemed that only perfection was acceptable, and of course, perfection on our part is never achievable. I see that as part of the pride issue in America, where being #1 seems to be the only acceptable position in life. We have been deceived in America to see anyone not achieving "number one" status as basically a failure – explicitly or implicitly. Never mind that you may be able to accomplish more in any given area of your life than 99% of the earth's population – there is only room for one at the top. How absurd!

I now realize that by degrading my abilities, I have thereby insulted God by not always giving him the glory and honor He deserves for exalting me in many ways. I may also have actually held myself back from accomplishing more than I could have and should have by subconsciously limiting myself based on my imagined inferior station in life. I hope my experience will help you see how you may have inadvertently limited your goals or achievements through an inaccurate picture of yourself.

Presently, I have learned to spend more time giving God glory and thanking Him for successes in every area of my life. Just as with you, God has blessed me with talents and abilities to share with others and to bring happiness in my own life. Humbly acknowledge your talents and abilities as gifts from God. Humility is simply living with the realization that everything you are and every good thing you have is a gift from God. You have done nothing to get your talents and abilities – you were born with them, gifts from God. How you use them reveals your attitude toward those gifts – whether you pridefully take credit for your accomplishments and use them self-centeredly, or you confidently acknowledge God as your source of every blessing and use what He has blessed you with to bless others.

The US Army and Technical College

God was especially kind to me while I was in the military, and exalted me in several ways – from being chosen a squad leader in my basic training company to achieving the highest scholastic score in our battery of academic tests in basic training to being Soldier of the Month representing the Military Police, and more. Surprisingly, none of those recognitions erased the feelings of inferiority I embraced as a child. They did cause me to consider that I was not as completely incompetent as I had come to believe.

Relating to my Military Police experience, I would like to comment on the phenomenon of carrying a gun and the feeling of power that accompanies it. I remember feeling a sense of power, confidence, and almost invincibility when I was on duty in my Military Police uniform with .45 caliber handgun strapped to my side. That causes me to understand to some degree why some young men born into an environment lacking love and stability – a dysfunctional environment where they have never felt respected or loved – may take to the streets with a gun or join a gang to feel some sense of power, respect, and acceptance.

All men have an internal need to feel respected. For those who have no connection to Christ or have only had negative influences in their lives, they might discover a gun brings them the false sense of respect they lack. The sad reality is that people do not respect them – they fear physical harm from them. Fearing for your life and showing respect are far from the same thing. If you are so emotionally beat down that you feel bottomed out, you might falsely believe a gun will gain you at least some sense of respect in your own mind if you have hardened your heart toward God and your fellow man. If you are reading this book and find yourself in that or a similar situation, Christ is your answer – not a gun. Connect with a God-fearing church to begin your healing process. Invite Christ Jesus to come into your heart, baptize you with His Spirit, and begin healing the damage that has been done in your life. Jesus loves you! Don't waste your life – it is too precious. You can trust Jesus with your life.

At the completion of my military service, I enrolled in a technical college. I received the Outstanding Student Award for my graduating class in Industrial Drafting and Technology, but once again I found a way to convince myself I didn't deserve it. Honestly; I still believe in my heart that there were other students more deserving than I was. I don't fully know why God chose to bless me with that award, but I give all the glory to God for exalting me in that way. I can only assume God chose to exalt me because I was seeking

Him and putting my trust in Him. God promises to exalt those who humble themselves before Him. God is not a respecter of persons. He will increasingly exalt you and bless your life, too, as you earnestly seek to develop your relationship with Him.

I have received recognition and honors through church, work, and sports, yet only in the past few years has God found ways to reveal my great worth to Him. I have known in my head that God loves me and values me all of my life, but my heart has sometimes struggled to believe it because of the trials in life that have caused me pain. It is quite natural to question why God would allow painful things to happen to you if you love Him and are seeking to live a life pleasing to Him. Through it all, I have found that we are indeed incredibly important and valuable to God. God does not bring negative circumstances into the lives of faithful believers. Satan – God's adversary and ours – manipulates circumstances in an attempt to cause us to forsake our belief in God. Satan tests us to see if we truly believe in our heart what we say with our mouth. I have recognized over time that each test has increasingly strengthened my faith as God comforted me in the midst of the trial and delivered me from each one. So as the apostle James said, *"Count it all joy"* because life's trials are designed to grow our patience and faith.

Married young – ill-prepared

My first wife seemed to reinforce my father's feelings about work. While we were dating, she and her parents came to my baseball and softball games and enjoyed them. After we were married and our first child was born, my wife felt that as a family man I should give up childish games and focus on what she considered important for a father to be doing.

As a young father, I tried to balance working two jobs to support the family, enjoy a night of sports during the week and some week-end tournaments, fulfill commitments at church, and meet the physical and emotional needs of my wife and children. When my children were pre-school age, I also enrolled in night classes to work toward a mechanical engineering degree per my wife's encouragement. I have found being a father and husband to be daunting tasks and you seldom feel appreciated. That is why if you are currently single, or a married man without children, I strongly urge you to seek counsel from an older Godly husband and father, and perhaps other outside sources, to prepare you for what to expect in marriage and child-rearing to help the process go as smoothly as possible for you. Make sure you seek mentorship from a mature Godly man because there are ample ungodly, selfish men who will give you all the wrong advice. Any advice you receive should be equipping you to be a better father and husband. If it is not, it is not from God and should be avoided.

As I said earlier, we are all flawed and damaged in some way and to some extent. We are selfish and prideful by nature. We all have preconceived ideas of how others should behave and what marriage relationships should look like based on the examples of parents, friends, and relatives. Being selfish by nature, the pride in us tends to make us think our vision of marriage is more valid than our wife's vision. Men – our pride many times prevents us from admitting we have flaws. Our pride can prevent us from seeking the benefit of counseling or mentoring from mature Godly men. Men – we are not always right, and our wife is not always wrong. If you want a happy marriage you will want to humble yourself and work together with your wife. Together with God's help, you can develop a healthy and fulfilling marriage.

I was married at the age of twenty to my fiancé who was seventeen. Like most young people, we thought we were more mature and ready for life than we were. In fact, I was naïve enough to think marriage would be like a continuation of dating; only we would get to sleep together. Well, after twenty-six years, three hundred and thirty days, our marriage ended, and marriage was not like dating.

I am not going to elaborate on our marriage's demise because that is not important for you to know and because it probably followed closely the pattern of most other marriage collapses – many little disappointments and unkind words over years of marriage that were never dealt with properly. Based on my experience, I recommend that you get marriage counseling early and get it as often as needed to keep your marriage healthy. The tendency is to pridefully think you can work through everything by yourself, believing that only weak people go to see counselors, psychologists, or psychiatrists. Either that or you believe things will just work out, which they seldom do without assistance. You may even believe from your experience that all married couples live in turmoil so you decide to just buck up and survive as best you can. God instituted marriage for our benefit. Marriage should be pleasurable and enjoyed so I encourage you to put in the necessary work to develop a friendship with your wife that will grow and prosper.

Since men and women tend to think differently and have different perspectives by design, you and your wife can easily get stuck in a bitter rut of thinking you are right and the other is wrong, getting so focused on your hurt that you no longer see your spouse through loving eyes. Because of unresolved hurts, you can begin seeing your wife through eyes of bitterness. When operating in bitterness, you will likely view your wife as your enemy and problem, losing all reason and sensibility to rationally and lovingly work through your differences. As numerous songs say, "Love is the answer." God also says love is the answer. God instructs each of us to love our wife tenderheartedly and unconditionally as He loves His bride (the Christian church). We may need outside assistance to accomplish that.

Seeking marriage counseling seems to be more of an issue for men than women. Most men seem to suffer from this machismos pride that causes them to feel they don't need counseling. If you can bring yourself to admit you are not perfect, you will position yourself to make gains toward becoming a REAL man. If you continue thinking you have it all together and know it all, you will never reach maturity. In that stubborn state of pride, you will find yourself continually missing out on blessings that naturally come with a humble walk with Jesus, your fellow man, and your wife.

Called by God to teach

I remember even as a little child wanting to be a pastor or minister for God, but with my low self-image, never thought that a possible reality, especially when I discovered you needed a college degree and seminary school to become a pastor. And remember, I hated school.

God called me to start teaching Sunday school when I was around thirty years old. I had endured a particularly stressful few years and had sought comfort in God's Word. After starting a family, buying a house, and spending time struggling to make ends meet, I began diligently searching for comfort and strength in God's Word. After reading through the entire Bible, the Lord called me to teach youth Sunday school. I was terrified at first because of my feelings of inadequacy and insecurities, but soon settled in and found that God had gifted me to teach and relate well to youth.

I thank God for the faithful women serving in so many capacities in most churches, but we need more men who love God to influence our children in a Godly direction. I learned to love Jesus, and I learned about Jesus through mostly women teaching Sunday school, but my dad and other men influenced my life's direction more. Women were the nurturers, but men were my examples. We naturally tend to pattern our lives after men that we look up to and respect – especially our fathers. There is a natural inclination in each of us to want our father's love and acceptance. Our daughters also look to fathers for proper guidance and acceptance, so as a father, don't think you are only a role model for your sons – daughters are watching and also need your love and acceptance to be emotionally healthy.

It is easy for a young man to pattern himself after the wrong kind of man if he does not have a solid Godly father example in his life to follow and receive instruction in Godliness from. Youth need to see that God is important to you and that you know His Word. Make an effort to realize how important you are as a man and father to your children's maturing process. You are vital!

Called by God to lead

Teaching Sunday school gradually led to serving in various leadership capacities. As my faithfulness and love for God became apparent to leaders within the church, I was asked to serve in a number of leadership capacities over time. Assuming leadership roles all began with seeking help and comfort through God instead of seeking worldly avenues for comfort and relief. Common worldly avenues of temporary comfort and relief include alcohol, drugs, porn, sex, or even over-indulging in hobbies and activities. What God has done for me and through me in leadership capacities proves to me that God will exalt and use anyone who loves Him and is committed to serving Him. It is not about us. It is about surrendering our hearts to the Lord Jesus and allowing Him to work through us, trading our pride, fears, and insecurities for faith and blessing.

If you want to be a REAL man, it all starts with surrendering your will to God. Acknowledge Him as your Lord and Savior, read and meditate on His Holy Word continually, and diligently seek a closer relationship with Him.

The painful divorce

When our son was a senior in college and our daughter was a freshman in college, my first wife and I divorced. It was the most painful event in my life, and yet brought tremendous inner peace to me because the arguing was over. I now know why God hates divorce. The pain of tearing a family apart through divorce, and its effects on children, no matter what the age, cannot be realized until after the divorce. I will never know the full toll the divorce took on my children because no one can truly put themselves in someone else's place and feel things exactly as they do. I will forever regret putting them through that pain.

After years of reflection on what happened to cause our divorce, I realize I contributed to the downfall of our marriage in many ways, just as my wife had. For years, I had difficulty not putting all the blame on my wife, but it wasn't all her doing. It takes two to make or break any marriage. We married too young. We did not get the counseling we needed early on. By the time we sought counseling, I guess neither of us had the patience or the real desire to work through the reconciliation process to heal the hurt from twenty-six years of damage.

Before a divorce, we can try to visualize the consequences and outcome, but until we actually go through with it, there is no way to fully understand the devastating effects. That is why I recommend counseling early and often if you get off to a rocky start or run into bumpy roads along life's way. Divorce should never be considered an option except in very rare cases of abuse or infidelity where the offending person does not want or intend to change their behavior.

I believe the basic roots that cause nearly every divorce are selfishness and pride – only thinking of what's in it for us. This may be the case of one or both of the spouses. Whether you have one loving selfless spouse and one selfish prideful spouse, or if you both suffer from selfishness and pride, the outcome is usually the same – misery for you both and unhealthy training for your children. I also believe that by the time you come to the point of even considering divorce, you have lost hope and built up so much anger and bitterness toward your spouse that you cannot think clearly. Anyone at the brink of divorce will likely need considerable time and counseling to keep the marriage together and make it healthy again. Having been through a divorce, I recommend you take the time to work through the healing process to avoid the divorce if at all possible.

If you have children, you have a great responsibility toward them, and God takes that very seriously. In fact, Jesus said that if you offend (mislead, badly treat, etcetera) little children, it would be better for you if they tied a great stone around your neck and threw you into the ocean. Therefore, take great care in the decisions you make that affect your wife and children.

Marriages need forgiveness and grace to grow and become healthy. It takes a genuine love and concern for your spouse to make a marriage healthy and strong. As long as either of you is only concerned with what you are getting out of the marriage, not what you are putting into the marriage, you will never have a satisfying marriage. In fact you will never have any healthy relationships with that kind of attitude. A good marriage, a good family, a good relationship of any kind requires a selfless attitude – being willing to forgive abuses against you that you don't deserve. Jesus said we must forgive as He has forgiven us or God the Father won't forgive us. To be healed, healthy, and whole, forgiveness and self-lessness are required. There is no other way, so work at developing a forgiving and gracious spirit.

A second chance

After divorcing, I did not intend to marry again. I had no desire to date. I just wanted to enjoy the peace and solitude that singleness brought. My college graduate son was living with me at the time, so I didn't feel lonely, and my daughter was living with her mother not too far away so I was able to see her quite often during the summers and by visiting her at college during the years following our divorce. There came a time, however, when I realized I did not want to spend the remainder of my life alone. My son is a volleyball referee, and as he advanced in ranking, he spent increasingly more week-ends out of town refereeing. It was during one of those week-ends the realization hit me.

During the fourteen months I spent alone with my son before meeting my current wife, I prayed often and shed a lot of tears seeking God in this matter. If there be a right woman for me, God would have to bring her to me because I wasn't going looking again. I found that love could be very painful, and I didn't want to go through that again. I even asked God for a specific sign if the right one came along. But I reiterated to God that I was not going looking – He would have to bring her to me, which He graciously did.

Now concerning tears, I know there is an old adage that says "men don't cry," but I will tell you that REAL men do cry. I once heard a famous U.S. Army general and war hero say in an interview that he didn't trust a man who didn't cry. Don't be afraid of showing your emotions. Jesus was more man than any of us will ever be, and yet we find Him weeping on a number of occasions out of love and compassion. So don't believe that worldly prideful non-sense about men not crying or showing emotion. If a man refuses to cry or show emotion, it reveals the depth of his pride, and we will discover as we continue that God resists the proud. God exalts, gives grace, and blesses the humble, so you decide if you want to fight God or get in His blessing line.

Even though the Lord brought my current wife to me, because of unresolved emotional damage, we ended up going to marriage counseling early in our marriage. That was a real blessing and breakthrough for me. Through marriage and individual counseling,

I have reached a place where I am confident in my relationship with God and realize in my heart how much He loves me. His perfect love continues to free me from pride – the enemy of our peace and contentment.

When you surrender your pride, you will find that you are not easily offended no matter what is said to or done to you. That sense of peace and security comes only with a deep heart-felt knowledge of God's love for you. God's love sets you free to enjoy others and overlook their faults and to accept the fact you aren't perfect either, but God loves you anyway. Bad days will come to test your faith, but God's Spirit will give you the strength, wisdom, and understanding you need to persevere. God's mercy and grace will sustain you so you can enjoy His gift of inner peace in the midst of each battle.

The path forward

Maturity does not come automatically and it does not come easy. Maturity comes as we seek God for direction and actively focus our attention on ministering to the needs of our wife and those around us. We cannot mature if we keep our focus on our wants and selfishly seek to satisfy our own desires. Peace of heart and contentment come from God as we seek to supply the needs of our wife and the people God brings into our path on a daily basis. As you seek to serve, others you will find God fulfilling your needs and the desires of your heart without you having to acquire them through your own natural means. This truly is a mystery. I can't explain how God does it, but it is one of God's principles that you can rely on.

Your maturing process may lead to marriage and individual counseling, which can be helpful in revealing your true self and calling in life, as well as root causes for any emotional issues you may be dealing with. Counseling seldom gives you all your answers – it principally leads you to a solution path. The love and goodness of God through Christ Jesus is the ultimate solution to every ailment, the only solution that heals your heart, mind, and soul.

Once you have identified the particular hang-ups and issues that keep you from enjoying God's inner peace and contentment, you are then able to focus on turning those burdens over to Christ Jesus who promises to care for you. A Christian counselor, psychologist, or psychiatrist can be indispensable in helping you understand yourself and why you respond the way you do in certain situations and relationships. I highly recommend professional Christian-based counseling to keep you and your relationships healthy. Secular counselors may also help you in understanding some of your behaviors, but they will lack the Christian worldview that will bring you to the source for complete healing – the love of God through Christ Jesus.

Ultimately, it is when you finally realize in your heart – not just your head – how deeply God loves you that you will experience freedom from fears and worries. That is when the abundant life becomes a reality. With the knowledge of God's love firmly planted in your heart, you will understand that He will provide, protect, and prosper you in every way as you learn to acknowledge Him as your God and Savior, trust Him as your Good Shepherd.

Seek the Lord continuously through prayer, reading His Word (the Bible) daily, fellowshipping with mature Christians, and attending church at least weekly. These things will help you overcome the selfishness and pride that cause friction, fear, and bitterness to creep into your heart and steal your joy and peace.

The road you are traveling right now has been influenced by many people in your life for good and bad. Depending on how much you have been influenced by God and Godly people versus non-believers and worldly people has predominantly determined your situation at this very moment. Hopefully, reading a snapshot of my story has caused you to reflect on your own life and see where you need to make some changes or improvements.

I was fortunate and blessed to grow up in a loving and caring family; even so, I developed many inaccurate ways of thinking and reasoning because we are all flawed and come short of the glory of God. You may have grown up in an abusive home, or other caustic environment. We all have had different experiences in life, but the thing true for all of us is that we are flawed, our environment is flawed, and we all need to surrender our wills into God the Father's hands, acknowledging our need for Him to enter our hearts and give us the power through His Spirit to overcome the world and live a life of inner peace and contentment.

You may be on a good road but need assistance climbing to the next level. You may be on a prideful road and need to learn the importance of humility and how humbling yourself before God and man can bring you the peace, success, and contentment you are seeking but have been unable to attain through worldly methods. You may feel inferior and need to discover just how much God loves you and that you are not worthless – you have great value in God's eyes, so much so that He became a human being and died to pay your sin debt. You may be sailing through life without any problems and feel you have no need for God. If that is you, you are on the most dangerous ground of all. Walking pridefully through life feeling like you have no need for God is the ultimate sin that separates you from God. God only reveals Himself to and blesses those who humble themselves before Him and acknowledge Him as their God.

Lasting peace and contentment are only available through Christ Jesus. He is the one who paid the price for you to receive eternal life and a blessed life on this earth. As the Bible says, *"humble yourself under the mighty hand of God, and He will exalt you in due season."* Don't let Satan convince you that you have no worth to God. And please, do not let him convince you that you can do it all on your own and have no need for God. If that is your current situation, I pray that God would open your eyes to see that He has truly provided every good thing in your life, including your talents and abilities.

Nothing you have done is unforgivable. In fact, whatever you have done or will do has already been forgiven through the shed Blood of Christ on the cross. To receive that forgiveness, confess your sin and acknowledge your need for God. Ask Him to come into your heart and change you. The moment you surrender your will to God, He comes in to begin the perfecting process. The Bible reveals that God is *"eager"* to be compassionate to everyone – He just waits for us to humble ourselves and ask Him to come in and take up residence. Go to God with a heart of gratitude and see if He won't come running after you to provide for your every need, giving you every good and perfect gift that only He can provide. Trust Him. Seek Him. Thank Him. He cares for you.

I have met a lot of men in my life – good, bad, and ugly. The biggest problem men have, in my estimation, is machismos pride. We tend to blame Eve in the Garden of Eden for the downfall of man and deceiving Adam into eating of the forbidden fruit. Personally, I doubt she had to do much convincing. I think he grabbed that forbidden fruit and started eating when tempted with the invitation to be like God. Ironically, he was already like God – having been created in God's image. What the devil actually tempted him to become was a prideful reject like he was. Satan, also called Lucifer, was cast out of heaven for his pride, thinking he could elevate himself above God.

Pride caused the downfall of man and initiated every negative human condition we have experienced since that fall. Pride is what keeps men from seeking help. Pride is what keeps men from admitting they aren't perfect and have limitations. Pride is what keeps men acting like immature five-year olds when they are fifty years old. Pride is what leads men to want to take over the world and rule in dictatorships through oppression. Pride is what keeps the world in a mess and it is caused primarily by men. Women have their faults, but they tend to be more focused on feelings, keeping the peace, and trying to reconcile relationships. Men's pride is what primarily causes all the devastation in the world.

Your story

What's your story? What wrong teachings and behaviors have you adopted as your own through influences of family, friends, or environment? What career or job profession desires have you suppressed and abandoned because of the direction others have steered your life toward?

Perhaps you were the school bully who boosted your self-esteem by picking on those smaller, weaker, or more timid than you. Many times, this behavior can be propagated by a father who thinks the only way to solve problems is fighting or bullying others to get your own way. Now you go through life intimidating others to get what you want, or to feed your ego.

Perhaps you are the pampered child who was never disciplined and never told no. You got everything you wanted, and now you whimper, whine, and throw temper tantrums to get what you want, selfishly just thinking of yourself because the attention has always been on you. The slightest thing that doesn't go your way causes you to get angry and storm off.

Perhaps you are the physically and emotionally abused child who was beaten and belittled by a mother or father who learned that pattern of living from their parents. Now you abuse your own wife and children because you haven't learned there is a better way.

Either that or you avoid intimate relationships because you fear being abused and rejected again.

Perhaps you are the man who was brought up in a Godly home where the discipline, reward, and love system performed perfectly as God intended. Yet, because Godly behavior caused you to stand out as being different as a child, you rebelled against that Godly upbringing to fit in more with your peers, struggling between doing what you knew was right and doing what would cause you to be more acceptable in the eyes of certain peers.

Maybe you were a gang member who hated other gangs and authorities and fought against them. Fighting out of blind hatred without even knowing why you hated them. Maybe you are still a gang member who is either living in blind hate not knowing why you hate, or you have matured to a point where you want to get out but are afraid of the consequences of leaving the gang.

Maybe you were the farm boy who made fun of city kids, or a city kid who made fun of farm boys because you were different. To boost your self-esteem and pride, you ridicule those who you may even esteem as being above you. Usually, this is the case in belittling behavior. Those who feel inferior slander and belittle those they consider superior to themselves in an attempt to build up their own self-image.

Perhaps you were the timid soul who was ridiculed for not being more macho or manly. Usually, this means that the emotional abusers are immature males who think you have to act like macho morons to be manly.

The point is we all have a story, and we are all flawed and emotionally damaged in some way. I hope after reading those scenarios, you realize at the root of all interpersonal relationship problems is pride – wanting to feel important and have control over others or at least over your own circumstances. Sooner or later, if you haven't already, you will realize that you have control over very little. About the only thing you do have control over is how you choose to react to life's situations on a daily basis.

What now?

No matter what your circumstance today, today is the first day of the rest of your life. If you are traveling the path you know God has prepared you, I congratulate you. Travel that path with joy and fervor and thanksgiving to God, looking for ways to bless others as you go.

If you are in a job or traveling a path that you hate and provide you no joy or satisfaction, then diligently seek God for His direction. Ask God to open the right doors for you. And remember to keep your spiritual ears and eyes open because as the Lord brings people your way with suggestions and contact information, or puts His direction in your heart Himself, God leaves the decision to you. Even though God provides open doors for you, He will not generally push you through them. You will have to make a choice. When God brings a blessing that involves change, you will be left with the decision to move out in faith or remain in your current circumstance. Many times, people out of fear of the unknown choose to remain in a miserable situation because it is a known quantity, rather than move out in faith toward the unknown, even when they know in their heart the new direction is the answer to their prayer.

It takes courage to move forward in a new direction, severing old relationships if necessary. It is not always easy or comfortable overcoming fears of tackling the unknown. God, when taking His people into new lands, told them throughout the Bible not to fear. He "commanded" them to be strong, of good courage, not to fear, nor be discouraged because He would be with them, never leaving or forsaking them.

It is important to remember that even though God gives us something, we still need to do our part, which sometimes means fighting for and pursuing what He has given us. Case in point is when He gave the nation of Israel the Promised Land in the area the current nation of Israel resides; although, what God gave them was larger than what they currently inhabit. Regardless, God told the leaders of Israel and the people of the Israelite nation that He had "given" them the land, but they would still have to go in and fight the nations currently living in the land, destroy them completely, and take the land. He also said He would go before them to drive out the enemy nations in the land. So we see that there are three parts to receiving God's blessings. Part 1 is His promise to give it to us. Part 2 is our believing Him and following His instructions – fighting for it at times if necessary. Part 3 is God fighting for us on our behalf – we never do it alone.

Remember that when you are faced with a difficult life changing decision. After you have prayed about it and are convinced in your heart you have received an answer from God that aligns with His will, then move forward with courage knowing that He will be there fighting right along with you to bring it about. There will usually be work involved in achieving or gaining any good thing because we appreciate more anything that we put effort into getting, even when we know it is a gift from God. So be strong. Be of good courage. Diligently follow the path God has set before you and you will reap the benefits God has prepared for you along that path.

Chapter 2

The process to REAL manhood

Micah 6:8 (NKJV – *emphasis added*)
*"He has shown you, O man, what is good; and what does God require of you but to **do justly**, to **love mercy**, and to **walk humbly** with your God?"*

*W*hen considering humility, I believe there is a tendency to envision weak and timid people. Nothing could be further from the truth. Truly humble people are strong and confident. After defining humility from Webster's Dictionary, I'll give you examples of humble people who have defined greatness.

Humility (humble)
Marked by meekness or modesty in behavior, attitude, or spirit
Unpretentious
Lack of pride
Showing deferential or submissive respect

Deuteronomy 12:3 (NKJV – *emphasis added*)
"Now the man Moses was very humble, more than all men who were on the face of the earth."

God used Moses to deliver millions of people from slavery in Egypt and lead them for the next forty years through a wilderness where they were completely dependant on God for their daily needs. God also entrusted His laws, precepts, and commandments to Moses to teach His chosen people, the Israelites-Jews. Moses was so close to God because of his humility that God talked with him as a friend, face to face. In Deuteronomy 12:7-8, the Lord says about Moses, *"He is faithful in all My house. I speak with him face to face."* I think you will agree it requires a REAL man to lead millions of whiny, stubborn people forty years through a wilderness where you are dependent on God for daily existence.

Since we have the documented journey of the Jews' continued waffling between faith-obedience and disbelief-disobedience, I think we have tended to unduly criticize the Jewish people. The Jews' story recorded in the Bible is our story-every one of ours. They did not have the benefit of Christ's once and for all sacrifice or the indwelling of the Holy Spirit. We owe our faith, our Christian beliefs, and our very opportunity to enjoy a reconciled relationship with God to the Jews. Of course, it is God to whom we owe everything, but He provided our opportunity through the Jews. Therefore, I encourage you to embrace a love for the Jews, Jerusalem, and Israel. They are still, and always will be, God's chosen people. God formed an everlasting covenant with them that He will bring to fulfillment.

Next I draw your attention to the Lord Jesus Christ.

Matthew 11:29 (TLB – *emphasis added*) Jesus said, *"Come to Me and I will give you rest-all of you who work so hard beneath a heavy yoke. Wear my yoke – for it fits perfectly-and let Me teach you; for I am gentle and humble, and you shall find rest for your souls; for I give you only light burdens."*

Jesus the Christ endured suffering, beatings, floggings, rejection, and humiliation for our sake and never once complained. He obeyed His Father's will to the death. That demonstrates the strength of true humility. Human pride is selfish and self-centered, tending to produce hurt and division. Godly humility is strong and tends to promote healing and reconciliation.

Our most destructive trait

A trait every man is born with through the inheritance of original sin is a need to feel respected. We all have, to some degree, a desire to be recognized and complimented to feed our ego so we feel important and good about ourselves. This is pride and is the essence of our fallen nature-the need to feel important, recognized, and in control of our lives and circumstances. From my experience, and from the feedback I have received from other men through the years, we especially want this from our wives, whether we always realize it or not.

Humbling ourselves is a process

Our pride is often easily offended and angered when we don't sense the respect from others we feel we deserve. For husbands, this seems to be most pronounced with our wife. When Adam and Eve rebelled against God, it not only caused a rift between God and man, but also between husband and wife. Jesus said a man's enemies would be in his own home. Living in harmony with the one we are united with for life is often our greatest challenge, but also brings the greatest rewards when we mature our emotions and learn to love mercy and show grace to our wife.

Since we are all at various stages of emotional and spiritual maturity, some react more maturely to offenses against them than others do. When we truly humble ourselves before God and walk in His ways, we increasingly take less offense as we grow to put more confidence and trust in God, our great Shepherd, not ourselves, our spouse, or our own natural abilities. The first step in humbling process is admitting that we are prideful and selfish. Then, through the power of the Holy Spirit, we resolve to continually humble ourselves. As we humble ourselves, inner peace and contentment become an increasing reality for us.

As I draw closer to God and as He continues to increase my wisdom and understanding, I increasingly realize that the curse of pride that propelled man into the free fall from God's grace continues to be our most basic obstacle in life-the one that causes strife and contention. Unfortunately, I believe very few people recognize their own pride and selfishness. But none of us have trouble recognizing pride in others. We have such a need through our fallen nature to feel good about ourselves (self-esteem) that we have a very difficult time seeing through our façade to see our faults and admit we are not perfect. Everything within our human nature seems to cling to its pride.

I want to clarify God's humbling process. In the Bible, we find overwhelming evidence that we choose blessing or curse. God lays out two paths for us to choose from. One leads to God's blessings. One leads to the curses inherent in disobedience. In essence, we humble ourselves by turning away from God. If we continue seeking God with all our heart, mind, soul, and strength, He continues to bless and prosper us as He has promised. If we choose to walk our own path in disobedience and pride, He withholds His protection and blessings. Most accounts of pronounced judgments, especially in the Old Testament, reveal that God simply withholds His protection and allows us to reap the natural consequences of forsaking Him. His Testimony also makes clear that He longs to be compassionate and will forgive and prosper us as we repent and return to Him.

Now, to begin humbling ourselves so we can enjoy God's protection and provision, we must model our thinking and behavior after our Savior. Jesus was tortured, rejected by his own brothers through much of His earthly ministry, spit on, beat, insulted, and worse yet, He never lost his peace because He firmly planted His focus and trust in His Father. He found His worth and strength in God His Father-not in Himself (His human abilities), or others' opinions about Him. God manifested (clearly revealed) in the flesh through Christ Jesus endured all of those things for the joy set before Him, which was reconciling His relationship to man. Jesus said He never did anything He did not hear or see the Father do. We experience the same peace, security, and contentment as we learn to do only what we hear and see the Father do-living in perfect obedience, loving mercy, and forgiving offenses against us. We do as Jesus revealed on the cross when He said, *"Forgive them Father, for they know not what they do."*

To maintain inner peace, you must mature to the point of consistently forgiving others for offenses against you. Work each day to surrender pride and seek to walk humbly with God and man. Pray for those who persecute you out of ignorance, and pray for your enemies out of pity that they might come to know the love of God in their own lives. Pray that God would continue to teach you how to love Him and others with the same sacrificial and unconditional love He operates in. Chances to be offended will come, but you need not take the offense. God's Word makes it clear we are to do everything within our power to seek peace and correct interpersonal conflicts, so choose to do the right thing. Choose to forgive.

Respect versus Pride

As you consciously begin weaning yourself from pride, you will find your peace, contentment, and prosperity in emotional health, physical well-being, and finances continue to increase. Freedom from pride brings you into a right relationship with God and man.

Living in pride leads to anger and bitterness. Bitterness leads to fretting. Fretting leads to self-absorption and self-pity. Wallowing in self-pity causes you take your eyes off God, who is your source of blessing, and place your eyes firmly on you and your problem, thereby hindering God from blessing you. This cause and effect relationship is true because God will only bless you with what you "believe" He can and will do for you. If you turn away from God through unbelief, which is what worry and fear are, then you prevent God's blessings from flowing to you. As God's Word says, *"It will be unto you according to what you believe."* I might add we need to believe in our heart. We can flippantly say we believe a lot of things, but our actions (fruit) reveal what we believe in our heart. If we say we trust God, but we obviously live in pride or fear, then we are lying to ourselves, and the truth is not directing our life.

This truth was confirmed in Jesus' home town. The Bible reveals that Jesus was able to perform few miracles in His hometown of Nazareth because of their unbelief. He managed to accomplish healing only a few sick people. Many places throughout Scripture reveal the truth that God will do unto us according to our faith (belief). Respect for God reveals itself through faith and obedience to God, and our respect for God results in a blessed and prosperous life. Doubt and disobedience, which are nothing more than disrespect for God, result in curses (lack of blessings).

Observe your surroundings daily and you will realize your physical and financial circumstances don't steal your happiness, contentment, or peace as many believe. Neither do other people's negative words or actions toward you. Many of the financially poorest and most physically and mentally challenged people display incredible joy, while some of the richest people with no obvious problems or lack of any kind display discontent and misery. This is just further evidence that peace and contentment are an inner spiritual matter that has little to do with our physical circumstances or how people treat us.

Pride is all about us. Pride wants others to notice us and how great we are. Our pride is easily offended when people don't notice us or acknowledge our self-imagined greatness or position the way we want them to. Respect, on the other hand, is something people do to us. People show respect by honoring us for acts of kindness, generosity, goodness, helping in times of need, and etcetera. Respect is gained through selfless outward focused service to our families and our fellow human beings. Respect is earned and essentially a recognition by others of our worth and value to them. Pride is an inward focused selfish trait that wants everyone to recognize and serve us. This is a very important distinction.

When we feel offended by others not paying us proper respect by our estimation, we are really indicating our pride was hurt because someone did not treat us the way we felt we deserved. This nasty trait of pride caused Satan's expulsion from the heavenly ranks and causes our expulsion from the good graces of God, our families, friends, and society. None of us like being around a person acting out in pride; and more times than not, that person may be you or me. So make a practice of humbling yourself. As you grow in spiritual maturity, you will continually be humbled as you realize how good God is and how bad your fallen human nature really is. That is when real life begins-when you realize in your heart that God loves you in spite of yourself.

Affects of daily decisions and expectations

We make decisions daily that affect our life's direction and the lives of others in some way. Therefore, I encourage you to mentally monitor the effects of each decision on others. Imagine how your decisions will affect your spouse, your friends, your church, your employer, your workmates-whoever it may be. Knowing how others' decisions have and do affect you emotionally, physically, and financially, you should be equally conscious of how your decisions affect others.

Rid yourself of prideful expectations for how others should treat you. And when you are presented with a chance to feel offended, find the strength to resist so you can maintain your inner peace. If you take the offense, you will find yourself moving into anger, self-pity, and bitterness-things that do only harm to you and deteriorate your relationships.

There are evil men who simply do evil things because they have chosen to abandon God. They literally do not recognize the difference between good and evil any more. They have hardened their heart to the point where they care nothing about others. They are acting out of the worst depths of human nature and depravity. Most men act badly through their spiritual and emotional immaturity-unable or unwilling to exercise Godly self-control. We may all have moments where this is our situation. For evil men, pray that God would soften their heart to see their need to accept Christ. For those of us in the continually maturing process, pray that God would continue to draw us into a more mature faith, increasing wisdom and understanding so we can come to a greater knowledge of God's love and share that with others in our own unique ways.

Humbling moments

You can only come to God as He draws you, and He will draw you because He desires that all come to a saving knowledge of Jesus the Christ. God is full of love, and He desires your love. Therefore, when you feel that gentle drawing, submit to God. Confess the sinful nature you feel at that moment. Confess the need and desire you feel to have Christ come into your heart and change you. Those are defining moments in your life. At those moments, you have a choice to make. You can acknowledge the need and desire you feel in your heart to reach out to Him, or you can suppress it and continue down your own path.

Because of God's great love, He provides many opportunities throughout our lives to come to Him. He prompts us through circumstances, traumatic events in our lives, friends and relatives, and many other ways. If we continually reject those invitations, however, we will increasingly harden our hearts toward God making it more difficult to recognize the truth of God. That is why it is so important to accept God the Father's invitation when He draws us in our hearts.

Grow Up

<u>1 Corinthians 13: 11 (NJKV – *emphasis added*)</u>
"When I was a child, I spoke as a child, I understood as a child, I thought as a child; but when I became a man, I put away childish things."

Normally, when we think of a child, we probably picture a person who is young in age. However, Jesus even called His disciples little children, so the term child can apply to us at any age, because we will always be in a maturing process.

<u>Mature / Maturity</u>
Having attained the normal peak of natural growth or development
Having attained a final or desired state usually after a period of ripening or processing
Taking place at the proper time

<u>Childhood</u>
The early period in the development of something

<u>Child</u>
One who in character or practice shows strong signs of the relationship to or the influence of another (as a disciple of a teacher: A child of God)

Have you ever been told to grow up? Growing up, or maturing, applies to many relationships in our lives. We mature in our relationship to our Lord, our spouse, our peers, our families, our church, and many others. Sometimes, we continue to mature in some relationships more quickly than others for a variety of reasons. If we experience emotional trauma in one of our relationships, we may emotionally disconnect (build walls) and turn our attention to maturing relationships that are not causing us pain. We may pursue activities and hobbies that bring us pleasure so we can avoid those relationships we struggle with. Unfortunately, that means we go through life incomplete and lacking because we close ourselves off to relationships that, if matured, would bring us increased joy and fulfillment.

The ultimate source of help to mature in all areas of our lives is God's Holy Spirit. Psychologists and psychiatrists can offer us much help to understand and deal with our mental and emotional anguishes, but complete healing only comes from the Lord because it is our spirit and soul (heart, mind, emotions) that ultimately need healing. Only the Lord can complete the healing process that brings inner peace.

Just as our physical bodies go through a natural maturing process, our emotions and spirit must mature. If we stop maturing in any area of our lives, we will stop short of the full potential that God has created us to reach. We reach spiritual and emotional maturity by continually seeking to grow closer in relationship with the Lord, seeking His will and direction for our lives. By continually seeking, we allow the Holy Spirit to guide us and increase our wisdom and understanding. With that wisdom and understanding, we become more effective relationship builders. If we don't fully mature in all areas of our lives, we short-change ourselves and others in our lives.

Here is one example to illustrate why a person might quit maturing. Think of a young child who cries to get what he or she wants. When a baby is born, he or she doesn't know how to communicate, so if they are feeling uncomfortable or hungry, they cry as a natural reaction because they are unhappy and want relief. As that child matures and learns to speak, he or she begins verbalizing requests. This is the point where the word "no" is usually introduced to them. Since they are not accustomed to being told "no," their natural reaction is to cry to get what they want because they have become accustomed to getting what they want whenever they cried. At that point, if the parent gives into their crying to appease them, they quit maturing and continue crying to get what they want whenever they are told "no," playing the child well into adulthood at times. Some people are still whimpering and whining to get their way well into old age because no one has taken a firm stand with them during their lives by sticking to their "no" when it was appropriate. If the parents are strong enough emotionally and spiritually themselves to deal with their young child's rebellion, that child will mature to the next level of maturity.

Also, consider the young bully who intimidated his peers physically or verbally throughout his adolescent and teen years to get his way. As time went on, his peers became afraid of him, so they would give him what he wanted to avoid verbal or physical abuse; it simply became easier to give in and then avoid him. Eventually, you all grew up and graduated from high school. You are now free from the bully. However, that bully has now been programmed to go through life intimidating people to get his way. If he continues his bullying behavior, he will likely wind up in jail, dead, or in a situation where he is finally forced to deal with his immaturity.

Judging maturity

Immaturity can be a habit perpetuated by associating with immature friends. Sometimes high school buddies who live in the same area after high school continue in their high school behavior long after they graduate because they refuse to mature. They may get married, have children, and have responsible jobs, but when they get together with each other, they tend to act just as immature as they did in high school. This could be the result of emotional trauma in other relationships, as I mentioned earlier. They may try holding on to some period in the past that was particularly pleasant for them as they avoid dealing with emotionally painful struggling relationships. Avoiding the maturing process short-changes everyone involved, so if you struggle with important relationships, I encourage you to get the help you need to continue the process and enjoy the benefits that come with maturity.

We judge maturity based on behaviors. Jesus said we would know a person by their "fruit." Fruit is another word for habit or behavior.

Matthew 7: 16-20 (NKJV – *emphasis added*)
"<u>You will know them by their fruits</u>. Do men gather grapes from thornbushes or figs from thistles? Even so, every good tree bears good fruit, but a bad tree bears bad fruit. A good tree cannot bear bad fruit, nor can a bad tree bear good fruit. Every tree that does not bear good fruit is cut down and thrown into the fire. Therefore by their fruits you will know them."

<u>Habit</u>
Condition, appearance, attire, character, disposition
The prevailing disposition or character of a person's thoughts and feelings: mental makeup.
settled tendency of behavior or normal manner of procedure
A behavior pattern acquired by frequent repetition or developed as a physiological function and showing itself in regularity

Even though hanging on to the past may seem comforting at times, we should seek to mature and move on. We are going to live the rest of our lives in the future whether we like it or not-not the past-so purpose in your heart to be strong and courageous in your pursuit of maturing into the man God has created you to become.

The work of the Holy Spirit

The Holy Spirit is our source of maturity, sometimes speaking directly into our hearts and minds, but oftentimes by leading us to another person, book, song, church, or other source of help. Jesus promised the gift of the Holy Spirit to all believers when He left this earth and said the Holy Spirit would lead us into all truth. Without the Holy Spirits wisdom teaching us, we will rely on the world's wisdom, which God says is foolishness. The Spirit of God is the only source available to mature you in every area of your life. If you are a born again from above believer, learn to listen to that still small voice. If you are a non-believer, listen to that calling in your heart when you feel a compulsion to receive the Lord as your Savior or feel led to a particular church-God is calling you unto Himself when you feel that urging.

John 14: 15-17 (NKJV – *emphasis added*)
"If you love Me, keep My commandments, and I will pray the Father, and He will give you another Helper that He may abide with you forever – the Spirit of truth, whom the world cannot receive, because it neither sees Him nor knows Him; but you know Him, for He dwells with you and will be in you."

John 16: 12-13 (NKJV – *emphasis added*)
"I still have many things to say to you, but you cannot bear them now. However, when He, the Spirit of truth has come, He will guide you into all truth; for He will not speak on His own authority, but whatever He hears He will speak; and He will tell you things to come"

You cannot fully understand God or His will for your life without the Spirit of God living inside you. If you want to understand God and His will for your life, you first must accept Jesus as your Lord and Savior, receive water baptism in His name for the remission of your sins, and receive the gift of His Spirit. His Spirit will then teach you and mature you emotionally and spiritually, giving you wisdom and understanding.

Without a growing relationship with the Lord, you will be looking to the world for direction in your maturing process, but the world in general is quite immature in its relationships. The world's immaturity is evident through all the fighting, hatred, and immoral behavior displayed daily. We all need the help of the Holy Spirit. So if you have not already, surrender your will into the Lord's hands today. Invite Him into your heart to be your guide and teacher. Then enjoy your maturing process as He continues to perfect you into a REAL man for the remainder of your life.

Qualifying yourself for God's blessings

Throughout the Holy Bible, God uses qualifying "if" statements with all His promises and covenants. He says every time that if we do something, then in return He will do as He has promised. Your knowing God and growing in your knowledge, understanding, and wisdom are conditional on your obeying His commandments. *Jesus said that if you love Him you will obey Him*-obedience is proof of love. Your material, emotional, physical, financial, and all other blessings are conditional on your commitment to follow and obey Jesus.

There seems to be a serious misunderstanding amongst many in the body of Christ concerning this matter. Many believe since we were washed clean in the Blood of the Lamb, we no longer must concern ourselves with living holy. If you walk into any given bar or casino around the world, you are as likely to find professing Christians as you are non-believers. This should not be. The Bible clearly states our salvation is a free gift that cannot be earned, but even that gift is conditional in a sense. Salvation is a gift from God freely offered, but its benefit to each of us is conditional upon our accepting that gift and allowing the Holy Spirit to clean us from the inside out. Receiving salvation goes beyond ritualistically acknowledging Christ as God and Savior; even Satan and his demons acknowledge that. You must surrender your will and allow the Spirit of Christ to enter your heart and steer your course. Becoming a REAL man filled with peace and contentment and successful in every area of life depends on you making some serious choices.

Few Godly men

Admittedly, we are all at different stages in our faith walk, but I have met few men that display a dedicated effort to mature their relationship with the Lord. Many seem to simply involve themselves in a church to hang out with friendly and sociable men working within areas or activities they enjoy, not because they truly care about furthering God's kingdom or growing closer to God. But a church member's maturity depends, to a large extent, on the maturity of the church and the quality of the teaching they receive.

Throughout my life, I have attended churches of varying denominations as a visitor and have noticed a tremendous variation in spiritual maturity and fruit produced. I have encountered churches so full of pride and arrogance they produce very little Godly fruit because God resists the proud. I have seen mature churches growing and producing mature Christian men and women who continually expand God's kingdom through various means. I have also encountered congregations so filled with fear and void of faith that they live in constant fear of disasters or financial shortfalls overtaking them, clinging to a fragile hope that everything will be okay.

Human nature being what it is, we are typically drawn to those like us. If we are immature and resist the sometimes painful process of spiritual and emotional growth, we will likely gravitate to immature churches engaged in gossip and avoiding responsibilities, blaming everything that goes wrong on others. That is what immature people do. If we are seeking God with our whole heart, mind, soul, and strength, we will gravitate toward a church comprised of mature Christians who are doing His will where we can grow and produce more fruit.

I have heard men say they only go to church because their wife makes them. I have known others who attended church and got involved because they either enjoy the notoriety they got or because they enjoy hanging out with men with similar interests in a friendly environment. I have encountered Christian men getting into a corner telling dirty jokes at church like junior high boys in a locker room. Our families, the church, and the world desperately need mature Christian men who truly love God and are seeking to live holy lives with grateful hearts for what God has done for them through the Blood of the Lamb, Jesus the Christ, on the cross at Calvary.

Ephesians 5:1-7 (NKJV – *emphasis added*)
"...be imitators of God as dear children. And walk in love, as Christ also has loved us and given Himself for us, an offering and a sacrifice to God for a sweet-smelling aroma. But fornication and all uncleanness or covetousness, let it not even be named among you, as is fitting for saints: neither filthiness, nor foolish talking, nor coarse jesting, which are not fitting, but rather giving of thanks. For this you know, that no fornicator, unclean person, nor covetous man, who is an idolater, has any inheritance in the kingdom of Christ and God. Let no one deceive you with empty words, for because of these things the wrath of God comes upon the sons of disobedience. Therefore do not be partakers with them."

Commitment and maturity accompany humility

1 Corinthians 3:1-3 (NKJV – *emphasis added*)
"And I, brethren, could not speak to you as to spiritual people but as to carnal people, as to babes in Christ. I fed you with milk and not with solid food; for until now you were not able to receive it, and even now you are still not able; for you are still carnal. For where there are envy, strife, and divisions among you, are you not carnal and behaving like mere men?"

1 Corinthians 3:16-20 (NKJV – *emphasis added*)
Do you not know that you are the temple of God and that the Spirit of God dwells in you? If anyone defiles the temple of God, God will destroy him. For the temple of God is holy, which temple you are. Let no one deceive himself. If anyone among you seems to be wise in this age, let him become a fool that he may become wise. For the wisdom of this world is foolishness with God. For it is written, 'He catches the wise in their own craftiness'; and again, 'The Lord knows the thoughts of the wise, that they are futile.'"

From my observations, every individual and every church is at a different level of spiritual maturity, and therefore, we see varying fruit (deeds and good works) produced by each. For those who are fully committed and diligently seeking God for wisdom and understanding, we see growth and prosperity-individuals and churches. For those who simply accept the gospel, they get into a church where they are happy just socializing and being saved-remaining baby Christians; we see very little spiritual development or fruit produced. In fact, those who stay at this baby level of faith are typically judging and condemning other Christians who don't see everything their way and judging non-believers in the world for their behaviors instead of evangelizing them through the love, kindness, and compassion of Christ. The Bible says the goodness of God leads to repentance and salvation-not our self-righteous judgment and condemnation of others.

I point that out because we need mature Christian REAL men to lead their families, churches, communities, and nation. Without spiritually mature leaders and men, we end up with violence in streets, bankrupt communities and governments, families overspending their means, rampant divorce rates, fornication, and all the other forms of evil that are so prevalent in the world. We need men especially who will commit to being REAL men by dedicating their lives to growing in their relationship to God-seeking wisdom, understanding, and knowledge from the only wise God who can provide those to us.

The outcomes of the world's perverted wisdom should be obvious to everyone by what is happening in our world today. But only those seeking Godly wisdom are even able to recognize the foolishness of worldly wisdom. As the Bible says, "*Godly wisdom is foolishness to the world, and worldly wisdom is foolishness to God.*" Since worldly wisdom is in direct contrast to Godly wisdom, if you are depending on worldly wisdom, you will never see the light of Godly wisdom and will continue to walk in darkness.

Men; I cannot stress this enough. To live a peaceful and content life, you must seek God for His wisdom, leaving your old worldly habits and worldly wisdom behind. Being born again from above is a literal rebirth of the spirit. That is when you begin to grow in Godly wisdom and understanding.

Your level of maturity when you are born again from above, and what natural intelligence and wisdom you were born with, decide how much you have to offer your wife, children, the body of Christ, and society at large at the time of your salvation. You may come into the body of Christ able to be an immediate contributor. Or you may enter as a babe needing to ingest as much Biblical instruction as you can to lead you into a mature walk with God. Either way, your life will be eternally changed after acknowledging God as your Savior, confessing your sin, and asking Him to come into your heart to beginning the changing process.

Pride – the great divider

A humble and wise person brings healing to relationships, unity to organizations, and mentors others to mature them emotionally and spiritually. In contrast, proud and arrogant people tend to breed hatred, animosity, and division among people, damaging relationships, creating disunity, and stunting the emotional and spiritual growth of others. Therefore, to be a REAL man who is part of the solution instead of part of the problem, a humbling experience resulting in a broken spirit and contrite heart may be necessary.

Proverbs 16: 5-7 (TLB – *emphasis added*)
"Pride disgusts the Lord. Take my word for it – proud men will be punished. Iniquity is atoned for by mercy and truth; evil is avoided by reverence for God. When a man is trying to please God, God makes even his worst enemies to be at peace with him."

Proverbs 13: 10 (TLB – *emphasis added*)
"Pride leads to arguments; be humble, take advice and become wise.

Proverbs 18: 12 (TLB – *emphasis added*)
"Pride ends in destruction; humility ends in honor."

Proverbs 16: 18-20 (TLB – *emphasis added*)
"Pride goes before destruction and haughtiness before a fall. Better poor and humble than proud and rich. God blesses those who obey Him; happy is the man who puts his trust in the Lord."

Proverbs 26: 12 (TLB – *emphasis added*)
"There is one thing worse than a fool, and that is a man who is conceited."

Pride is a natural part of human nature. In fact, pride defines human nature. Pride prevents us from developing healthy relationships with God and our fellow human beings- that is why we should humble ourselves, or God will eventually humble us by allowing us to self-destruct.

Prideful people put others on guard. Pride is rebellion against God. By definition, pride means you think more highly of yourself than you do others, so when you approach others with a prideful attitude, it results in a natural emotional barrier between you. Pride causes others to be unreceptive to your advice and guidance.

A humble person, on the other hand, is not a threat to anyone because he does not pretend to be more than he is and actually esteems others above himself. A humble person is truly interested in the welfare of others; therefore, others are usually more open to share with them and are receptive to what they have to say.

When you need help or advice, who do you go to-a person puffed up with pride, or a humble person? Would you share your insecurities and deepest fears with a prideful person? Why or why not? Would you share your insecurities and deepest fears with a humble person? Why or why not? Do you tend to show respect and honor to conceited people or humble people? Why?

Proverbs 26:4-5, 9 (TLB – *emphasis added*)
"When arguing with a rebel, don't use foolish arguments as he does, or you will become as foolish as he is! Reply to a fool as his folly requires. A rebel will misapply an illustration so that its point will no more be felt than a thorn in the hand of a drunkard."

It really serves no purpose to argue with a fool or to try teaching him or her anything. He or she really has no interest in learning anything from you. A fool is a fool and enjoys doing foolish things. A fool may actually define the epitome of pride mixed with ignorance. There may come a time, however, when that fool is humbled to the point where he or she is ready to listen, and that is when you will have the opportunity to witness God's goodness to them. Until then, avoid trying to reason or teach a fool bent on doing foolishness; otherwise, your conversation may end in a foolish argument with no purposeful conclusion.

Proverbs 19: 8, 11 (TLB – *emphasis added*)
"He who loves wisdom loves his own best interest and will be a success. A wise man restrains his anger and overlooks insults. This is to his credit."

Proverbs 22: 4 (TLB – *emphasis added*)
"True humility and respect for the Lord lead a man to riches, honor and long life."

We have talked much about pride and humility, and earlier we defined humility. Now we define pride from Webster's to better understand the behavior and attitude God resists, and, in fact, says He hates.

Proud
Possessing or showing too great self-esteem, overrating one's excellencies
Arrogant, haughty, lordly, presumptuous

Arrogant
Having excess pride

Pride
A sense of one's own worth, and abhorrence of what is beneath or unworthy of one, lofty self-respect, noble self-esteem, elevation of character
That of which one is proud, that which excites boasting or self-congratulation, the occasion or ground of self-esteem, or of arrogant and presumptuous confidence
Proud or disdainful behavior or treatment, insolence, or arrogance of demeanor, haughty bearing and conduct, insolent exultation

Conceit
Too high an opinion of one's abilities, worth, or personality; vanity
Holding too high an opinion of one's self

Do you think too highly of yourself? Do you think yourself to be a prideful person? To find out, let me ask you a few questions.

When you meet other men, do you mentally compare yourself to them? Do you see their shortcomings and get a feeling of superiority toward them in some respect, be it physically, emotionally, intellectually, or spiritually? That is pride. When you are in conversation about any subject, do you feel the compelling desire to add your opinion because you are certain you know more about it than they do? That is pride. When you have a conflicting viewpoint over religion or politics, do you find yourself arguing to prove you are right and they are wrong? That is pride.

How might a humble person react in those same situations? When meeting other men, a humble person might notice their strong points and consider how they are a benefit to humanity. When in a conversation and feeling they had input, a humble person might casually interject added information with no feelings of superiority, just feeling that he or she would like to help them receive a deeper meaning. When conflicting with someone on religious or political viewpoints, a humble person might graciously acknowledge the difference of opinion and change the subject.

James 4:5-10 (NKJV – *emphasis added*)
"Or do you think that the Scripture says in vain, 'The Spirit who dwells in us yearns jealously"? But He gives more grace. Therefore He says: 'God resists the proud, but gives grace to the humble.' Therefore submit to God. Resist the devil and he will flee from you. Draw near to God and He will draw near to you. Cleanse your hands, you sinners; and purify your hearts you double-minded. Lament and mourn and weep! Let your laughter be turned to mourning and your joy to gloom. Humble yourselves in the sight of the Lord and He will lift you up."

Humble men are teachable. God can work with humble men to increase their wisdom and understanding. God can work through humble men to accomplish much good throughout the earth. If you want a good reputation, humble yourself before God and He will increase your wisdom and understanding in all things and exalt you in the eyes of your peers and superiors. As you become increasing more generous with your time and money and outward focused through humbling yourself, you will find God increasingly prospering you in every way so that you have more to share–spiritually, emotionally, financially, and through your increased knowledge in other areas.

Godly wisdom

We are admonished throughout the Bible to seek wisdom from God. To understand what God encourages us to see from Him, we again turn to Webster's Dictionary.

Wisdom
The effectual mediating principle or personification of God's will in the creation of the world

An intelligent application of learning

Ability to discern inner qualities and essential relationships

Exercising sound judgment

Wisdom indicates discernment based not only on factual knowledge, but also on judgment and insight

Proverbs 8:12-13 (NKJV – *emphasis added*)

"'I, wisdom, dwell with prudence, and find out knowledge and discretion. The fear of the Lord is to hate evil; pride and arrogance and the evil way and the perverse mouth I hate.'"

Wisdom characteristics as revealed in the book of Proverbs in the Holy Bible:

Wise men listen to instruction, thereby increasing their learning

Wise men–men of understanding–seek wise counsel and advice

Wisdom guards the paths of justice, and it preserves the way of the saints

Wisdom brings understanding of righteousness, justice, equity, and every good path

Discretion preserves you, understanding keeps you; these are gained through wisdom

Wisdom delivers you from evil and wayward women

A wise man loves mercy and truth

When you love mercy and truth, you also gain favor and high esteem from God and man

A wise man trusts in the Lord with his whole heart and does not trust in his own understanding

A wise man acknowledges God in all of his ways, and God in return directs his paths (Jeremiah the prophet recognized that man is incapable of planning his own life)

A wise man honors God with his possessions (bringing tithes and offerings to the church, and generously helping the poor and needy)

A wise man gladly accepts God's correction and discipline, knowing that it is benefiting him

Gaining wisdom and understanding makes a man happy

The Lord formed the earth and established the heavens through wisdom and understanding

Sound wisdom and discretion give life to our soul and grace. They cause us to walk safely without stumbling.

A wise man inherits glory

God blesses the house of the just man (wise man); the house of the wicked (ungodly man) is cursed

Getting wisdom is the principal thing (most important) along with gaining understanding

When you embrace wisdom, wisdom will exalt you and bring you honor

Chapter 3 in the book of James tells us *"wisdom from above is pure, peaceable, easy to be entreated, gentle, full of mercy, without partiality, full of good fruits, without hypocrisy."* If you walk wisely, "God's Spirit will lead you, and the Spirit will produce the fruit listed in Galatians 5:22-23: *"love (charity), joy, peace, long-suffering (patience), gentleness, kindness, goodness, faith, meekness (humility), and self-control."*

Fruit implies it is grown, which takes time. Jesus said a tree is known by its fruit; it takes time to grow trees and fruit. We need patience with ourselves and with each other since we are all trees (works) in progress. Demonstrating the fruit of the Spirit does not come naturally–it takes a REAL man to endure to the end, constantly growing into the Godly fruit-bearing tree that God desires.

God created us in His image. We rebelled against His authority and fell from grace. Christ's sacrifice has reconciled that relationship for those who accept it and begin walking in it through the power of the Holy Spirit. We, as believers, are branches connected to the vine of Jesus–we only grow as we stay connected to Jesus, absorbing nutrients from Him, learning from Him, seeking to draw closer to Him. Jesus is our source. Our spirit dies a slow death if we don't stay connected to Him.

The apostle James also informed us *God will gladly and generously give wisdom to anyone who asks for it, so if you truly want to be wise, ask God and He will make you wise*. Get over the idea that you can become wise on your own. Accumulating knowledge, college degrees, and worldly acclaim does not make you wise–it just increases the amount of knowledge floating around in your brain. I believe you will never be more intelligent than the day you were born. God preprogrammed you with likes and dislikes, talents and abilities. How you choose to use those talents and abilities determines whether you become a wise man or an educated moron.

Godly wisdom or worldly foolishness

We are all called by God and given certain talents and abilities to help the body of Christ; and by default, the rest of humankind. In my estimation the CEO of a company is no more important in God's eyes than the janitor who cleans up everyone's mess at the end of the day.

Think about it. God has gifted certain people with the intelligence and ability to start and run huge corporations for the benefit of the world and the employees who will come to work for that corporation. He has given others the ability and personality to stand at a production machine eight hours a day for forty years machining parts to make products that satisfy the needs and wants of people. Others are gifted with administrative abilities, engineering abilities, and etcetera. For any organization to function properly, fulfill its mission, and be successful, it needs all the parts working together in unity and harmony.

Our secular world system through human pride has set up economic systems that say people with certain God-given talents and abilities are more important and worth more money and compensation than others. Maybe there should be some differentiation in pay based on responsibilities and accountabilities, but I think most would agree the economic system is grossly disproportionate from top to bottom. The Bible also warns the rich to pay their servants (employees) fair wages. We can see through the large disparity between rich and poor that the rich are not fairly distributing their wealth for the benefit of their employees. Every working person deserves a livable wage, but it seems the trend is in the opposite direction. We are gradually eliminating the middle class to create a two-tiered system – rich and poor. This eventually leads to a country's demise.

If we had a world of all CEO's, they would be nearly worthless and likely accomplish very little on their own. God has given the heads of companies and corporations the ability to visualize and organize into a business to provide a product or service. They are able to bring all the pieces of the puzzle together to make a functioning organism of people. However, it is all the individual pieces of the organism that make the organization function. That is why no executive should ever feel puffed up about himself or herself, because they are simply using the talents God gave them for the benefit of other people.

Likewise, if we had a world full of janitors, engineers, administrative assistants, etcetera, we would not advance or do well either. No one should ever feel puffed up or ashamed of his or her position in life because we are all simply using what God has already given us. Everything we have is a gift from God and meant to benefit others as well as ourselves.

The foolishness of man

To further emphasize the foolishness of man, I want you to consider a few facts. Our human bodies are comprised of approximately two-thirds water and one-third dirt. The surface of the earth is composed of approximately two-thirds water and one-third dirt. We are made up of the very earth in the same general proportions that we walk on every day and depend on for food to keep our bodies functioning properly. Furthermore, we strive day-after-day to accumulate money to buy stuff created from this same earth and water to surround ourselves with stuff made from the same raw materials that we are made of.

We especially like things that are shiny and bright. Gold, silver, and precious stones draw peoples' attention. Yet these are just metal rocks or stones harvested from the same earth that we are made of. Those skilled in the area of marketing know full-well how to appeal to this *unregenerate human nature*. It is no accident that commercials seek to appeal to our pride and vanity, always promising to make us superior to others in some way to entice us to buy their product so we can achieve an image they are promoting.

It is no accident that places like Las Vegas and other destinations of morally corrupted values use so many colorful and shiny lights to draw attention – we are drawn to bright shiny objects. But those bright shiny objects never bring lasting happiness or contentment. It is better that we seek the brightest and shiniest object of all – the Glory of God in Christ Jesus. God is also called the Light and in Him there is no darkness. Jesus is the Light of the world and anyone who seeks him will never hunger or thirst in the spirit again. All the shiny bright objects in secular society are just distractions to keep you from the real thing – a life filled with the Spirit of God.

The peace, contentment, joy, and happiness the world promises to give you through the accumulation of money and possessions are all available through Jesus – the Savior and Redeemer of us all. It is only through a growing intimate relationship with Him that lasting peace, contentment, joy, and happiness are possible. I wish I had the power to give every human being an infusion of this knowledge and desire to love God, but God, in His infinite wisdom, decided to give you that choice because *loving someone is impossible without having the choice not to love them.*

If you seek God and His kingdom above everything else, He promises to give you all the other stuff the world seeks after as a gift – adding no sorrow with it. God wants a relationship with you. He loves you and wants you to love Him back. There is no other way to lasting peace, contentment, or prosperity.

Walking in humility

Imitating Christ in everything you do is at the core of walking humbly with God. Jesus the Christ had a deep reverence for His Father in Heaven. He said in one prayer that He never did anything He did not see the Father do, and He never said anything He did not hear the Father say. Christ accomplished that perfect obedience by delighting in His relationship with His Father and through the Holy Spirit who filled Him beyond measure.

That same Spirit comes to dwell in you to give you wisdom and power to live a Godly life after you surrender your will to God, not before. You may learn to act Godly on the outside, but God knows your heart, so you must surrender your will and your heart to experience God's full measure of blessing. Take a lesson from the next scripture verses giving Godly advice to the young pastor Titus.

Titus 1:15-2:2 (NKJV – *emphasis added*)
"To the pure all things are pure, but to those who are defiled and unbelieving nothing is pure; but even their mind and conscience are defiled. They profess to know God, but in works they deny Him, being abominable, disobedient, and disqualified for every good work. But as for you, speak the things which are proper for sound doctrine; that the older men be sober, reverent, temperate, sound in faith, in love, in patience;…"

Titus 2:6-8 (NKJV – *emphasis added*)
"Likewise, exhort the young men to be sober-minded. In all things showing yourself to be a pattern of good works; in doctrine, showing integrity, reverence, incorruptibility, sound speech that cannot be condemned, that one who is an opponent may be ashamed, having nothing evil to say of you."

Recall men in your life who you consider good men. What kind of qualities did they have, or do they have? Do they not exhibit Godly characteristics?

God puts knowledge of Himself in the heart of every human being. If we choose to walk away from God through pride to follow our own path, that knowledge will slowly leave us. The farther we walk away from God, the less we will want to be reminded of Him. At some point, we will become so blinded to the truth that worldly wisdom will make sense and Godly wisdom will not. That is the state of much of our world today – right has become wrong, and wrong has become right.

The first chapter in the book of Romans in the Holy Bible describes ungodly behavior and reveals that if you decide you do not wish to retain God in your mind any longer, He will give you over to your own path and perverted thinking. Then right starts becoming wrong, and wrong starts becoming right in your mind. That is because Satan is the ruler of this world and there is no truth in him. If you follow your own prideful path, there will be no truth left in you either, and that is when worldly wisdom seems right and Godly wisdom seems wrong. One glaring example of this perverted thinking is the acceptance and promotion of homosexuality in the world today. God's Word clearly says in numerous places that homosexuality is an abomination in His sight, but even many Christian churches today have fallen for Satan's deception concerning this behavior – all in the name of tolerance and trying to create one big happy society without following God's precepts and commands. This is nothing more than human pride – feeling we know better than God.

Let's look at some more Godly advice the apostle Paul gave his understudy, Titus.

Titus 2:11-14 (NKJV – *emphasis added*)
"'For the grace of God that brings salvation has appeared to all men, teaching us that denying ungodliness and worldly lusts, we should live soberly, righteously, and godly in the present age."

Titus 3:1-7 (NKJV – *emphasis added*)
"Remind them to be subject to rulers and authorities, to obey, to be ready for every good work, to speak evil of no one, to be peaceable, gentle, showing all humility to all men. For we ourselves were also once foolish, disobedient, deceived, serving various lusts and pleasures, living in malice and envy, hateful and hating one another. But when the kindness and the love of God our Savior toward man appeared, not by works of righteousness which we have done, but according to His mercy He saved us, through the washing of regeneration and renewing of the Holy Spirit, whom He poured out on us abundantly through Jesus Christ our Savior, that having been justified by His grace, we should become heirs according to the hope of eternal life."

Walking humbly with God means you realize you are His creation – He is the potter and you are the clay. You willingly submit to God's will and allow His Spirit to lead you, teach you, comfort you, and give you the power you need to fulfill His will in your life. Remember that God resists the proud but gives grace to the humble. I encourage you to submit so you can begin your journey down the abundant road of peace, contentment, and joy that God has planned for your life if you have not already made that commitment. He bought you with a price – the death of His only begotten Son – so you do not belong to yourself anymore. The sooner you realize that and voluntarily submit your life to God, the sooner you realize the blessings He has waiting in storage for you.

Ephesians 4:25-32 (NKJV – *emphasis added*)
"Therefore, putting away lying, 'Let each one of you speak truth with his neighbor.' For we are members of one another. 'Be angry and do not sin', do not let the sun go down on your wrath, nor give place to the devil. Let him who stole steal no longer, but rather let him labor, working with his hands what is good, that he may have something to give him who has need. Let no corrupt word proceed out of your mouths, but what is good for necessary edification, that it may impart grace to the hearers. And do not grieve the Holy Spirit of God, by whom you were sealed for the day of redemption. Let all bitterness, wrath, anger, clamor, and evil speaking be put away from you, with all malice. And be kind to one another, tenderhearted, forgiving one another, even as God in Christ forgave you."

Philippians 2:3-4 (NKJV – *emphasis added*)
"Let nothing be done through selfish ambition or conceit, but in lowliness of mind each esteem others better than himself."

Philippians 2:14-16 (NKJV – *emphasis added*)
"Do all things without complaining and disputing, that you may become blameless and harmless children of God without fault in the midst of a crooked and perverse generation among whom you shine as lights in the world, holding fast the word of life, so that I may rejoice in the day of Christ that I have not run in vain or labored in vain."

That is just a sampling of the wisdom and direction provided in God's Word, the Holy Bible. His Testimony is a gift to increase our understanding, wisdom, comfort, and knowledge of God's nature and plans. The Bible contains revelations of the future and end-times events so we can recognize the signs of the times and know that Jesus is coming soon. The Bible contains the spiritual food we need to feed ourselves daily to keep your spirit strong and healthy, just as we need to feed our physical bodies good food each day to keep them strong and healthy. ***Your spirit can no more go without reading and hearing the Word of God every day to be healthy than your body can go*** *without food to be healthy.* I encourage you to take advantage of this tremendous gift made available to you.

Make a practice of reading God's Word daily and spending time in prayer each day, communicating your thanks to God and presenting your requests. Realize God has a better plan for your life than you can ever produce on your own. Continue seeking God for wisdom and direction in life. God is faithful and dependable to fulfill your needs and give you the desires of your heart as you continue to seek a closer walk with Him.

Growing into a REAL man – concluding comments

The Bible makes clear that pride separates us from God – it is the complete anti-God state of mind.

You and I can never experience the peace, joy, success, and contentment that accompany a surrendered relationship to God without calling on the name of Jesus, admitting we are sinful beings in need of Him, and inviting Him to enter our heart to lead, guide, and perfect us, then going on to live life with a heart of gratitude and thankfulness for all He has done for us, is doing for us, and will still do for us.

As you continue seeking God, He will continually reveal more of Himself to you. God, as your Father, wants to also be your Friend. Just like developing any human relationship, to develop your relationship with Jesus takes time and effort. It requires spending time with Him, asking questions, sharing your deepest dreams and desires, and just enjoying His presence.

Since you are God's creation – unique among all humanity – only God knows how to satisfy your longings. As long as you pursue your own selfish ambitions and live in a prideful state primarily concerned with what you want, you will constantly face anxiety, discontent, disappointment, discouragement, as well as a multitude of other negative consequences of walking your own path. I know because I have struggled with this also. As much as I humble myself and seek to imitate Christ in everything I do, say, and think, I struggle with pride and selfishness like every other human being. But as I age and continue to seek God, the struggle increasingly lessens, and the benefits and blessings associated with following Christ continue to increase.

To become the REAL man that we all want to be deep inside, you need to live a humbled outward focused life of love. As you walk the Godly path of love, you will find yourself increasingly enjoying a more satisfying and content life as the Lord works in your life on your behalf. May God Bless you and increase you in every way so that you can be an increasing blessing to others.

Chapter 3

Marriage – God's gift to man

I have been married thirty-nine years of my life and have found marriage to be my most rewarding as well as my most challenging relationship. I purpose in this chapter to give you an understanding of God's intent for marriage as defined in the book of Genesis. I address many of the issues that cause strife in marriage and show how our changing societal culture contributes to that strife.

We start with God's first recorded thoughts on marriage and review definitions from Webster's Dictionary relating to the marriage relationship.

Genesis 2:18 (KJV – emphasis added)
"And the Lord God said, 'It is not good that the man should be alone; I will make him an help meet for him.'"

Help
To give assistance or support to
To assist in attaining
To be of use to: BENEFIT
To further the advancement of
To change for the better: MEND
Help, aid, assist are all verbs that are virtually interchangeable

Meet
To join in conversation, discussion, or social or business intercourse
To form a junction or confluence: follow or enter an identical course
To occur or appear together: UNITE
Helpmate
One serving as a companion, partner, or assistant

Helpmeet
Genesis 2:18 "I will make a help meet for him." (KJV)

Complementary definitions to helpmate include:

Companion
One that accompanies or is in the company of another
A partner or associate especially in a legal or formal relationship (spouse)
To unite in fellowship

Wife
Woman
A woman acting in a specified capacity
A married woman
The female of a pair of mated animals

Husband
Peasant owning his own land
A married man
The manager of another's property
To take care of, utilize to advantage, manage
To use sparingly or hold back for future use

As you ponder those definitions, I believe you will clearly see God's intent for marriage is reflected more in the definitions for help, meet, and helpmate than the definitions for husband and wife. God has created for each of us destined for marriage a woman to be our friend, companion, and soul-mate. As shown the commonality of marriage conflicts, infidelity within marriage, divorces, and the like, we see that the majority of us have not learned to embrace and appreciate the gift God has given us.

God's orderliness in marriage – the husband's role

God has assigned man the responsibility of being the spiritual head of his family and loving his wife unconditionally as Christ loves His bride (the church of believers), ultimately sacrificing His life for her (us). God instructs us to tenderheartedly consider our wife's needs above our own and sacrifice everything for her if need be. He warns us through His prophets and apostles to never treating our wife harshly. Instead, we are to treat our wife as the precious gift from God that she is.

Women are predominantly feelings oriented, and men are predominantly problem-solving oriented. Much conflict in marriage comes because husbands and wives do not attempt to understand the basic differences between men and women. Because of the fallen nature we inherit through sin, we as husband and wife have tendencies to try to mold each other into something more closely resembling our nature instead of seeking to understand each other's nature and viewpoint.

For example, most often when our wife dumps her feelings on us, she is not looking for us to solve her problems; she is just looking for a sympathetic ear. Our first inclination as a husband is usually to analyze her every word trying to formulate a solution to relieve her agony. I have learned that keeping our mouth shut and sympathetically listening is often the best thing we can do in those situations. If we offer advice when it is not wanted, it can cause our wife offense. Then we take offense because she is offended at our genuine desire to help make her feel better.

The Bible talks much about the tongue being an untamed evil. We learn in the Bible that the man who learns to tame his tongue has control over his entire body. Practicing speaking less and listening more can help you immensely in your marriage relationship.

I remember hearing somewhere that women are more interested in emotional stability than financial stability. In contrast, I believe most men are more interested in financial stability than emotional stability. As a husband and father, I seem to have a natural inclination to meet the physical needs of my family and provide what I consider a comfortable life and environment for my family. Seeing that women like things and seem to be shoppers by nature, I think we men can be deceived into thinking our wife requires more things to be happy. But buying more things and increasing financially will only make your wife happy if you are giving her the emotional stability she needs and wants more.

Money and stuff are no substitutes for being tenderhearted and considerate toward your wife. Things are no substitute for loving gestures, a tender touch, and soft kind words that tell your wife how much she means to you. For the health of your marriage, treating your wife as a fine fragile gift to be treasured and cared for is paramount. I think most men struggle with this because that is not the way we are generally wired. The world compounds this issue by giving us just the opposite message everyday, telling us through incessant marketing that we "must" buy and accumulate more things to be happy.

The world seems to predominantly teach men to act like macho morons to be manly. Only deceived women are looking for a macho moron, and when they get him, they are usually disappointed. Women need and want, even though they may not always realize it because of the world's deceptions, a tenderhearted, loving, Godly man.

Understand that the world promotes lifestyles and beliefs that are exactly opposite God's, and they package them to look very attractive. But as evidenced by all the chaos, broken relationships, and hurt permeating the world, we should easily recognize the world promotes false promises. To understand the true source of happiness, it is vitally important for you to read God's Word, the Holy Bible. The truth and path to a life of joy, inner peace, and contentment is found in God's Testimony – nowhere else. Also, connect to a church that will help you grow in wisdom, faith, and understanding. Develop friendships with mature Christian men who can help you walk the Godly lifestyle. If you do these simple things, you will mature in your relationships with God, your wife, your children, and your peers as you diligently seek God.

The effects of modern culture on marriage

We have often heard "it is a man's world." Men usually say it with pride, and women say it with disgust because it seems many of our post-feminist modern women now want to rule the world themselves now that they have experienced some of that power achieved through the feminist movement.

As stated in the Holy Bible, Satan is actually the ruler of this secular world. The Bible also reveals that, as believers, we are in the world but should not be of the world. As we live in this current world, we must choose between two paths – the path to Heaven and eternal life or the path to Hell and eternal death. Those are the only two choices. According to Jesus, very few will walk the road to eternal life – most will choose the broad road to eternal damnation. Our modern western culture is increasingly conforming itself to Satan's nature instead of God's nature. Through this conformation, we see increasing chaos in the world and even many Christians struggling to hold their families and marriages together. The world has rebelled against God through pride, deciding it knows better than God how to run His creation. It started with Adam and Eve. Their once perfect union was severed through their pride and rebellion against God, and that in turn resulted in their own prideful rebellion against God and each other.

The western world has increasingly become a unisex society which has caused much confusion regarding roles for men and women. In response to the perversion of God's intended order, we are naturally following a path of moral perversion and ultimately will reap the destructive rewards with more regularity and intensity until finally we as a society reach the bottom and hopefully call out to God again to intervene and save us from our prideful stupidity. This course of destruction is nothing new. You can read all about it in the Bible and history books. History continues to repeat itself because man continually resists and rebels against God – our Creator, Sustainer, and Redeemer.

God intends for husband and wife to work together in life as friends and companions. Men and women, for the most part, think differently, emotionally react differently, and generally have different interests. We are not created to be the same. We are created to be complements – like heads and tails on the same coin. But because of society's perversion of God's order, husbands and wives seem to increasingly seek control over each other instead of seeking to work together in harmony.

One of the byproducts of the feminist movement has also been increasing financial prosperity and education for women, which I applaud. These improvements in their condition seem to have also contributed to increasing conflicts between men and women and husbands and wives and to the increasing divorce rate and the amount of couples living together out of wedlock. As women have become better educated and financially independent, instead of putting up with physical or emotional abuse as they may have in the past when they had fewer viable options for supporting themselves, they now seem to leave marriages they may previously have endured because of their lack of options. But I don't believe their leaving is predominantly because of abuse today. I believe more often women leave marriages today for the same reasons men left in the past and still leave marriages today – they are dissatisfied and simply want something new. Prosperity brings with it many times unintended negative consequences.

We are witnessing declining individual and societal morals. As we have increased in financial and material prosperity, we have increased opportunities to act out the perverted intents of the heart that have always been there. As individuals increasingly act out the perverted desires of their heart and see no immediate retribution or punishment from God, it leads to a false security. Thinking we can pridefully do anything we want without experiencing God's punishment naturally leads to the false assumption that we need not fear God. As we keep pushing the moral limits and see no immediate retribution, we push the line a little farther until we find ourselves enmeshed in muddy moral decay and can no longer recognize our true condition.

To illustrate this fact, view popular movies beginning in the early 1900's through today. You will see how morals and behavior have degraded continuously one step at a time each decade over the past 100 years. You will see evidenced through popular movie media societies moral decline documented. Each decade, moral sensibility limits have been tested and stretched until society says enough-is-enough. Then as society became recalibrated to the new level of moral degradation, the limit was stretched again. This has happened gradually but repeatedly over the past century until we find ourselves in a moral cesspool and wonder how we got here.

That same gradual degradation has flowed into marriage relationships. Prosperity and independence give men and women a level playing field where each has more opportunity to follow their own path and justify it by society's increasing acceptance and tolerance of immoral behavior. As King Solomon in the Bible once wrote, *"There is nothing new under the sun. What is has been before."* Prosperity tends to bring with it a false sense of security and the feeling for many that we don't need God. We have everything we need and can live life the way we want. Read your Bible to see where that path leads.

The fact that women have more options and are not as dependent on their husbands for their livelihood anymore can lead men predominantly down two paths from my perspective.

The first path drives fear into the husband, knowing his wife doesn't rely on him financially. Recognizing this fact consciously or subconsciously, the husband lives and operates out of fear of losing his wife and perhaps the financial security by trying to cater to her every whim and demand. Or through fear he tries to control her through jealousy to prevent her from leaving. He won't be happy because he is operating out of fear, and she won't respect him or be happy for the same reason. Fear is a crippling force. When operating out of fear, it is often difficult or impossible to see the truth in the midst of the fog.

The second path leads him to operate out of love. He seeks to be the best husband he can be and enjoys the benefits of his wife's extra income and independence. He seeks to ensure his wife she is wanted and appreciated through tenderhearted gestures and words which should eliminate any inclination on her part to want for anything different. He respects her independence and sees her as a friend and companion rather than a possession he must aggressively try to hold on to for fear of losing her. I believe you can see how this is the better path to choose. Ultimately, we tend to either live out our lives in fear or love. There is very little middle ground between those two choices.

A man's responsibility to his wife in marriage

<u>Deuteronomy 24:5 (NKJV – *emphasis added*)</u>
"When a man has taken a new wife, he shall not go out to war or be charged with any business; he shall be free at home one year, and bring happiness to his wife whom he has taken."

We men are charged with caring for our wife as the weaker vessel – weaker in the sense of fine china or a very precious and delicate article, not in the sense of being inferior in any way. As I already pointed out, we are charged with treating our wife tender-heartedly and carefully considering her needs above our own. The success or failure of a marriage many times rests on the shoulders of the husband because God has assigned us the leadership role.

God created woman to be our helpmate, men. That means her main role is supporting us emotionally, giving us advice to help us stay on the right course, and helping us become what God created us to be – successful in everything we set our hands to. We are charged with loving our wife as Christ loves the church. If we don't treat our wives as we should – tenderheartedly with unconditional love – the Word of God says our prayers will be hindered. How we treat our wife very much determines the peace, contentment, and success we will experience throughout our lives.

Confusion reigns

God established marriage in the beginning, blessed that union, and designated it as the basic unit of society. After joining them as one (marriage), God told Adam and Eve to be fruitful, multiply, and have dominion over the earth. God created everything orderly. Today it seems man is still attempting to recreate God's order to fit his fleshly lusts. Instead of getting married, establishing a committed marriage relationship, and raising a family, we more often than not see young people fornicating before marriage and living together many times instead of making a marriage commitment. Instead of marriage before children, we now see with increasing regularity children before marriage. Through this perversion of God's established order, people ask why things aren't going better for them or why life is so hard. Life is so hard because we rebel against God's established order to do things our own way. Our human nature wants to be God and create God and the world in our image.

I believe my generation – baby boomers – has been a relatively poor example of commitment to our children and have been a cause of much of the perversion and disorder we are witnessing today. Our generation led the way to quickening moral decay with the free-love movement, increased drug use movement, increased cohabitation outside marriage, in-your-face sex everywhere you look, a do your own thing without regard for others mentality, and the list goes on. The quickening moral decay admittedly began much earlier, but our generation increased the downward spiral at an exponential rate. No wonder the younger generation of today is so commitment adverse.

Taking the spiritual lead role

No matter what generation we are born into, when married young it seems many men have not yet matured into the spiritual head of the household role they are intended to fill. Because of the man's immaturity, wives seem to many times act more like mothers than wives to their husbands. This, from my observation, can lead to a role-reversal that begins deteriorating a marriage. In a common scenario, because the immature pride in the man resents his wife treating him like a child from his perspective, he begins to withdraw to spend more time with his buddies, work, or hobbies so he doesn't have to be reminded by his wife that he is not meeting her expectations. By the time he matures to the point of being ready to lead, the damage to the relationship is many times done and roles are fixed. The wife has assumed a leadership role she was never created to assume and unlearning must begin. At this stage, anger and resentment many times reign, and neither the husband nor wife can think clearly to resolve their issues. That is a brief summarization of what sometimes takes years to develop but is not an uncommon theme in marriages.

When conflicts in marriage arise, the most mature men and women will seek marriage and individual counseling to resolve the conflicts so the marriage can continue to grow stronger. We don't have to live life bitter and resentful, but through pride, many men resist admitting they may have some flaws or emotional wounds that need attention. Women wanting to resolve interpersonal conflicts by nature are usually willing to seek help. But since women struggle with pride and vanity, it may be a struggle for the wife to seek and benefit from counseling as well. I personally believe we all have emotional wounds and misguided teaching acquired through life's experiences that need attention. It is no shame to seek help to overcome emotional damage that causes you to live without joy, peace, and contentment. I encourage you to seek whatever counseling will help you live the abundant life Christ died to give you. It is Satan who comes to steal, kill, and destroy our abundant life – don't let him steal, kill, and destroy your life and marriage!

Women are sensitive and prideful beings, too. Many times, she may react to her perception of your inability or unwillingness to take the lead by being bossy and nagging or turning to shopping or other interests if she is not getting the loving support she expects from you. I am convinced that it is stubborn, selfish, human pride that separates marriages. We all seem to get hung up focusing on the symptoms of the problem without getting to the root of the problem, which is pride and selfishness. Since we are prideful and self-centered beings by nature, both husband and wife have a natural tendency to focus on their own hurt and what they are not getting out of the marriage instead of focusing on the needs of the other and seeking to see life through the other's eyes. Since God has assigned men the spiritual leadership role, however, God holds us to a higher level of accountability in the formation of a successful and happy marriage than He does our wife.

Therefore, humble yourself before the Lord and surrender your pride – that is the one sin that separates you from God, your wife, and others more than any other. Then, if needed, seek individual and marriage counseling early and do it as often as necessary to steer you and your wife onto a healthy marriage track and keep you there. If you wait too long, it may take so long to heal the damage that you both give up and succumb to divorce. That is the tragic end to a prideful, selfish, and unloving standoff.

There is no shame in seeking help and direction through counseling. In my view, that is one of Satan's greatest deceptions in his effort to break up marriages and families – convincing men they are weak if they seek counseling when just the opposite is true. Fearing what others will think if you seek counseling is a weakness of pride and indicates you are more fearful of what man will think of you than you are interested in making your most important relationship (marriage) prosper.

God brings us a wife to help us become better men. We must commit to becoming strong Godly men by patiently and tenderheartedly persevering through the conflicts and struggles of adjusting that naturally come with marriage. If you can humbly endure the maturing process and resist speaking unkind words when you feel offended, then God can continue to prosper your marriage and family. Develop a tender, loving, forgiving heart. Be slow to speak and quick to listen. Practice acting out of love and not fear. Practice viewing life through your wife's eyes. Study your wife to see what is important to her. A happy wife makes a happy husband.

Effect of the curse on marriage

In the beginning, God made humankind in His image – male and female. Therefore, God encompasses the qualities and characteristics of the male and female whereas we – male and female – possess half of the puzzle. The intention for marriage is that husband and wife fit together as complements, working together to accomplish a harmonious and loving life together. But since the fall of man through rebellion against God, we often tend to pridefully seek to recreate our spouse into our spiritual and emotional image instead of accepting and enjoying her image.

Since men and women generally seem to be opposite in nearly every way – the way we do things, the way we think, the way we feel, the way we set priorities – we many times do not embrace and appreciate our differences to form a complete unit working together (one flesh) as God intends. Instead, we more often pridefully focus on our differences and fault each other for not being more like we are and thereby perpetuate the effects of the curse on our own well-being. Instead of enjoying happy spiritually and emotionally secure and thriving marriages as God designed us to enjoy, through our conforming to Satan's prideful nature, we struggle to unconditionally love our wife as we should.

Since the fall of humankind into sin, husbands and wives struggle to enjoy the differences that could benefit both by embracing God's marriage design – learning to complement each other instead of competing against each other in so many ways. This was just part of the curse realized through the fall of man into sin – enmity (deep-seated dislike and ill-will) developing between husbands and wives through accumulated hurtful words and acts. This enmity is made obvious through the percentages of divorces, illicit affairs, and spousal gossip that pervade everyday life.

Our prideful natures seem more often than not to attempt creating an environment around us that is exactly what we want it to be so we feel comfortable and at peace. We tend to all like things our way and are many times more selfishly concerned with our own comfort level and well-being than anyone else's – that is the ugly characteristic of human nature.

God's nature is completely giving, and that is the image he originally created us in. Satan's nature is completely selfish and prideful, and that is the nature we inherited from Adam and Eve's rebellion. The good news is we can now be restored to that original completely giving nature and enjoy the abundant life that comes with it. All it takes is an honest heart-felt calling upon the name of the Lord Jesus, confessing our sin by acknowledging our sinful nature, and asking Him to come in and start perfecting our heart toward Him, our wife, and everyone else in our life. That is how easy it is, but it is a lifelong process. Jesus referred to us as trees bearing fruit, and as you know, trees grow slowly and bear more fruit as they grow and mature.

The blame game

When Adam and Eve sinned, pride and shame entered the human race. As soon as they sinned, Adam's and Eve's spiritual eyes were opened and they felt ashamed, knowing they had sinned. Their first response was to blame someone else for their choice to disobey God and we are still doing it today.

The breakdown in the marriage relationship spills over into all areas of society. People blaming others for the poor choices they make and for the things that go wrong in their lives. Men and women blaming each other or the devil for just about everything that goes wrong for them. When Adam and Eve made the choice to disobey God, Eve blamed the serpent for convincing her to eat the forbidden fruit. Adam blamed God for giving him the woman. Neither Adam nor Eve wanted to take responsibility for their choice. As evidenced by all the divorces and frivolous lawsuits we see going through our courts today, it is obvious that we still do not want to take responsibility for our own actions and control our behavior. It is much easier to blame someone else for our pain and errors and, in the case of marriage, walk away from a relationship that was meant to last a lifetime.

The pride in us does not want to recognize or admit we are flawed. Nor does our pride want to forgive offenses against us. Our fallen human nature wants to deflect all of our imperfections onto someone or something else so we can remain feeling good about ourselves. Blaming is one way of shaming another person into giving you what you want. Shame-purposed blaming is never appropriate, but it happens in marriage as well as other relationships. And from my observations and perceptions, conflicts in marriage spill over into society and the workplace. I truly believe that if all married couples enjoyed harmonious, content marriages, we would see that behavior carry over to produce harmonious, content societies. Healthy marriages are the glue of society. It is obvious that our glue is dissolving, and our societies are dissolving along with marriage relationships.

Expectations

Jeremiah 29: 11-13 (KJV – *emphasis added*)
"For <u>I know the thoughts that I think toward you, saith the Lord, thoughts of peace, and not of evil, to give you an expected end</u>. Then shall you call upon me, and you shall go and pray unto me, and I will hearken unto you. And you shall seek me, and find me, <u>when you search for me with all your heart</u>."

It seems much of the pain we experience in marriage and life occurs because of unfulfilled expectations. As we view several definitions relating to expectation, try determining what you can do to avoid disappointment when your expectations are unfulfilled. And perhaps you need to examine yourself to determine how many unreasonable expectations you have. Since the marriage relationship is the most important human-to-human relationship we have, it is vital for your wife, children, and society that you learn how to live in love and harmony with your wife; expectations play an extremely important role.

Expect
To look forward with anticipation
To consider probable or certain
To consider reasonable, just, proper, due, or necessary
To consider a person obligated or duty bound

Expectation
The act or state of waiting
The mental attitude of one who anticipates

Anticipate
To consider in advance
To look forward to as certain

Disappointed
Defeated in expectation or hope

Disappointing
Failing to come up to expectations

We all have many expectations, some reasonable, some unreasonable. When our expectations are met, we may realize great satisfaction and joy. When our expectations are not met, we may experience immediate and severe disappointment and sadness. I think many people go into marriage with unrealistic expectations. I say unrealistic because I think many expect the dating feeling produced through hormonal overload (lust – not love) to last forever in marriage. A reality I have heard many times from many Christian sources says love is a commitment and deliberate action toward another, not a feeling.

While dating, I believe most of us are predominantly blind to the little imperfections in our future wife. In fact, we usually consciously or subconsciously attempt to hide our own little imperfections because we want our date or future wife to like us. We may fear that if they knew the real us, they would walk away. Since dating love can be more blind lust than real love, we may even think all those little things we don't like in her will go away after marriage, or we will be able to change her habits we don't like after marriage. It won't happen.

It is good and right to have expectations, but since we live in a fallen world that is full of evil and depravity, we will not always get what we expect. Sometimes we and others make poor choices that bring disappointment and pain. We will always have failed expectations because we live in a broken world filled with selfish people. We live in a world that God has created and is in control of, however, so when we seek Him with our whole heart, soul, mind, and strength, we can expect Him to bring us through each disappointment we face. God's Word says He will even protect us from accidents when we love Him and seek to obey Him. I know this to be true from experience. I can give you numerous examples of God's direct intervention in my life protecting me from accidents and negative consequences. People may disappoint us, but God never will if we earnestly seek to do His will and trust Him with our lives.

Disappointment and anger are sometimes appropriate reactions when our expectations aren't met. Sometimes when reasonable expectations aren't met, it leads us to promote a needed change in some behavior, law, or circumstance. The expectations we should avoid having are the unreasonable ones. It is unreasonable to expect our wife to always act the way we want her to. It is unreasonable to expect our wife to always make us happy. It is unreasonable to rely on our wife for all of our needs and wants. It is also unreasonable to think we can always make our wife happy.

When setting expectations, keep in mind, as the prophet Jeremiah said, ***"It is impossible for a man to plan his own life."*** It is comforting to know God has a plan for our life. We will only enjoy perpetual inner peace and contentment when we choose to walk the path He has prepared for us and completely trust Him with our life. If you humble yourself and patiently take things as they come – trusting in the Lord one day at a time – and let the Lord direct your life, you will live an increasingly content, peaceful, and joyful life.

The Lord promises us many things, and we can fully expect Him to deliver on His promises if we do our part by not setting ourselves up for disappointment with selfish or unreasonable expectations. God is faithful and will fulfill His promises to us – that is a reasonable expectation and one we can count on. Putting expectations on our wife or anyone else in our life to always come through for us or act as they should is an unreasonable expectation.

<u>Psalm 62: 5-7 (KJV – *emphasis added*)</u>
"My soul, wait thou only upon God; for <u>my expectation is from Him</u>. He only is my rock and my salvation: He is my defense; I shall not be moved. In God is my salvation and my glory: the rock of my strength, and my refuge, is in God."

I challenge you to make God your only rock of strength and depend only on Him for all of your needs and desires. He has promised to give you an expected end if you do, and that expected end is the fulfillment of the perfect plan He has for your life.

Take the sting out of your disappointments by realizing that your God loves you and wants only good for you. The Lord desires for you to experience His peace and live a satisfied life. Don't set yourself up for disappointment by unreasonably expecting people or things to satisfy what only God can satisfy – your need to be loved and accepted and safe.

Jesus said if we seek God's kingdom and His righteousness first, then our heavenly Father will give us everything we need to have a fulfilled and blessed life. Keep your expectations focused on God and His kingdom, and you will find yourself increasingly blessed with peace and contentment because your desires and expectations will line up with God's will, and He gladly gives "good things" to His children.

Love and enjoy your helpmate

Enjoy the wife that God has blessed you with. Quickly forgive offenses against you and treat her tenderheartedly as a fine and fragile gift from God.

Good marriages and relationships develop because each person involved is concerned more with what they are putting into the relationship than what they are getting out of it.

Since you can't control the behavior of your wife, nor should you since that is her job through the leading of the Holy Spirit, when conflicts arise, the best you can do is tell her how you were hurt by some particular action she took or words she said in a kind and gentle way. If she chooses not to change, your only option is to pray about it and readjust your expectations to accommodate the reality. Then trust God to work things out so your marriage continues to grow and flourish. As God works things out, you then will learn He is faithful and trustworthy. As time elapses, you learn that every trial or temptation you face is ultimately designed for your good, even if you can't understand it. So learn to count it all joy as we read in the book of James – learn to be thankful in all circumstances, knowing that God cares for you and will work things out as you patiently and cheerfully wait on him with your "mouth shut." I emphasize mouth shut because our tongue many times short-circuits God's effective working in our lives.

God provides us with a helpmate whom Adam named woman because she was a part of his own body. That is why the Bible says a man will leave his father and mother to cleave to his wife and become one flesh with her in spirit and closeness. God created us male and female to bond into a union of friendship, companionship, and closeness like no other human relationship – marriage.

Proverbs 18:22 (NIV – emphasis added)
"He who finds a wife finds what is good and receives favor from the Lord.*"*

Proverbs 19:14 (NIV – emphasis added)
"Houses and wealth are inherited from parents, but a prudent wife is from the Lord.*"*

I encourage you to develop a friendship with your wife and value her opinions. The odds seem to favor the possibility you and your wife have vastly different personalities, which can cause conflict until you mature emotionally to accept your differences. As you accept your differences and continue to mature emotionally, learn to embrace and appreciate your differences.

I once read a quote by an author unknown who said he had never learned anything from someone who agreed with him. Through pride, men and women routinely seek companionship with those who agree with them. It may be comfortable fellowshipping with only those who think and behave like you, but it will stunt your intellectual, spiritual, and emotional growth. One area of growth is available through your wife. Learn to value your wife's opinion and seek her advice on matters. As you begin valuing her opinion, you just may be surprised at what you can learn from her perspective. By valuing her opinion, you will likely cause her love, appreciation, and respect for you also increase over time. I want to emphasize that this takes time, so relax and enjoy the journey.

Marriage with Christ at the center

The marriage relationship is truly a mystery because when two people love and marry each other, they begin their journey into becoming one flesh. For the marriage with Christ at the center, it truly becomes a fulfilling and rewarding relationship like no other.

For Christ to be at the center of a marriage, He must also be the center of each spouse's life, however. If both husband and wife focus on loving the Lord and walking in His ways, they will tend to seek the best for each other and seek to be the best partner they can be. They will tend not to be self-centered, thinking only of what is in it for them; they will be seeking the welfare of the other as they seek to do the will of God. This takes time. Our inherited pride continues to battle our spirit for control. Even though the spirit is willing, the flesh is still weak and wants its own way, so the journey into oneness is truly a journey.

I do believe two people who do not believe in God might still have a rewarding marriage if they share mutual interests and have a satisfying sexual relationship. But I also know that a life with Christ at the center is much more rewarding and strengthened by the bond of Christ that lacks in a marriage void of that relationship. Relationships without Christ as the bonding agent are more fragile and likely to dissolve over issues that those grounded in Christ are able to endure through mercy, grace, and forgiveness. However, statistics bear out even professing Christians divorce at rates similar to non-believers. Therefore, we clearly see the battle within between our renewed spirit and prideful flesh that resists overlooking offenses against us is a powerful battle.

1 Peter 3:7 (NIV – emphasis added)
"Husbands, in the same way be considerate as you live with your wives, and treat them with respect as the weaker partner and as heirs with you of the gracious gift of life, so that nothing will hinder your prayers."

As I mentioned earlier, I have learned that in the original Greek, the word rendered weaker in this verse refers to a fine fragile possession that you cherish and guard from harm with great care. The verse in no way refers to women being inferior to men in any way. This was also made obvious through the definitions we read earlier pertaining to helpmate.

Ephesians 5:25-33a (NIV – emphasis added)
"Husbands, love your wives, just as Christ loved the church and gave himself up for her to make her holy, cleansing her by the washing with water through the word, and to present her to himself as a radiant church, without stain or wrinkle or any other blemish, but holy and blameless. In this same way, husbands ought to love their wives as their own bodies. He who loves his wife loves himself. After all, no one ever hated his own body, but he feeds and cares for it, just as Christ does the church – for we are members of his body. For this reason a man will leave his father and mother and be

united to his wife, and the two will become one flesh. This is a profound mystery – but I am talking about Christ and the church. However, each one of you also must love his wife as he loves himself…"

Godly men respect their wives and love them as much as they love themselves. Failing to love our wife unconditionally on a regular basis hinders our prayers as we read in 1 Peter 3:7. So, men – ask yourself, how is life going for you? Are you happy, content, prospering in everything you set your hand to? If not, one major reason may be in how you treat your wife. How are you treating your wife? For the dating single men, how you are treating the woman in your life? Are you treating her kindly and with respect? Do you value her opinion? Do you spend time seeking to bring out her God-given talents, abilities, and qualities? Do you look for ways to show her how important she is to you? One thing is certain. You will not experience a life of inner peace, joy, and contentment unless you treat the woman in your life with respect, honor, and love.

Malachi 2:13-16 (NKJV – *emphasis added*)
"And this is the second thing you do: You cover the altar of the LORD with tears, with weeping and crying; so He does not regard the offering anymore, nor receive it with goodwill from your hands. Yet you say, 'For what reason?' Because the LORD has been witness between you and the wife of your youth, with whom you have dealt treacherously: yet she is your companion and your wife by covenant. But did He not make them one? Having a remnant of the Spirit? And why one? He seeks Godly offspring. Therefore take heed to your spirit, and let none deal treacherously with the wife of his youth. 'For the LORD God of Israel says, that He hates divorce, for it covers one's garment with violence,' says the LORD of hosts. 'Therefore take heed to your spirit that you do not deal treacherously.'"

Treachery (treacherously)
Deliberate, often calculated, disregard for trust or faith
The act of violating the confidence of another, usually for personal gain
Full of guile

Guile
Astuteness often marked by a certain sense of cunning or artful deception – a trick
To reiterate God's concern for the welfare of the wife, and a husband's duty to love her, let's revisit the verse we read earlier from the book of Deuteronomy.

Deuteronomy 24:5 (NKJV – *emphasis added*)
"When a man has taken a new wife, he shall not go out to war or be charged with any business; he shall be free at home one year, and bring happiness to his wife whom he has taken."

Other Scripture verses further explain that a husband is responsible for seeing to his wife's needs and raising Godly children. God places much responsibility on the man, but as evidenced in the world today, too many men ignore their commanded responsibility. Too many men abandon their responsibilities when the going gets tough, leaving their children's mother to assume responsibilities she was never meant to endure. If you are willing to mature into a REAL man by willfully following God's instructions and precepts, you can enjoy an abundant life and incredibly fulfilling marriage relationship.

Men; it is easy to hurt people and live an ungodly, selfish, and prideful life, but that kind of life always leaves a deluge of hurt and societal damage in its wake. IT TAKES A REAL MAN to face up to his responsibilities. It takes a REAL man to stand firm when the going gets tough. It takes a REAL man to consider the needs of his wife, his family, his church, and society ahead of his own. It takes a REAL man to live life God's way.

God created us and has given us the rules for healthy relationships. We men need support and encouragement from our wife. From my own perspective, and I believe most men would agree if they were honest with themselves, we need the support, love, and encouragement of our wife to be healthy and strong and to accomplish more than we would on our own. We also need direction from our wife at times to make right decisions and should welcome her advice. Husbands and wives are partners – equal partners – with differing roles.

From a wife's perspective, I believe a wife needs the security of a Godly, loving, and caring husband to feel secure, healthy, safe, and whole. It is much easier for a wife to submit to the will and direction of a Godly, loving, mature, and caring husband. I also feel that a husband will do nearly anything for a wife who is caring, loving, respectful, and willing to support him emotionally. If we are willing to live within the bounds of God's rules and precepts, our relationships will continue to grow stronger.

Single – but considering marriage

If you're single but considering marriage, ask yourself why you want to get married and why you want to marry the one you think you do. I would suggest that for most young men, the main attraction is physical and one of the biggest reasons for thinking of marriage is sex. You may like doing many things together, but my experience says that most young men pick a partner based on physical attraction and feelings rather than through prayer, careful thought, and considering what qualities are important to them. In fact, this is probably even the case among older men.

While dating, couples may enjoy long talks, going to movies or amusement parks, eating out at nice restaurants, going for long walks, and etcetera as they seek to know each other intimately. Seldom during this process do couples give appropriately serious thought to what comes after marriage. Being physically attracted to each other and enjoying each others' company is certainly important, but it is just one of many facets to consider in the one you plan to marry.

When dating, find out as much as possible about yourself and your girlfriend. What is important to her? What is important to you? What habits of hers irritate you that you think you will fix in her after marriage? Newsflash! You will not fix her habits after marriage, and the harder you try, the bigger the wedge you will drive between you. What qualities in her irritate you and are impossible to overlook? Conversely, ask yourself what qualities or habits you have that probably irritate her and consider how those might affect your marriage. Are you willing to change things about yourself to accommodate her comfort level? These are important factors to consider before marriage.

Before considering marriage, first pray. Ask the Lord to direct you to the wife He has prepared for you. Once you believe you have met the right one, seek pre-marital counseling and take the recommended pre-marital tests to determine your compatibility. My understanding is the pre-marital tests reveal with high accuracy which couples have a high probability of a successful marriage and which ones will almost certainly end in divorce. Carefully consider the advice you receive from pre-marital counseling in deciding whether or not to marry.

It seems that we many times choose a personality completely opposite ours when we start dating, especially when we are young. One explanation I have heard for this is we are looking for someone to complete those parts of us that are lacking. For instance, if we are by nature quiet and introverted, we may tend to pick someone who is talkative and outgoing. Unfortunately, after marriage, those differences can be aggravations that drive couples apart if they do not learn to accept their differences.

I think a better explanation for being attracted to an opposite personality is that we, as humans, seem to be often drawn to new and exciting things. Choosing someone with an opposite personality may seem exciting for a while, but after the novelty wears off following some period of time in the marriage, sources of difference can become sources of irritation.

More than likely there will be some things your chosen mate does that you would prefer she did a little differently – that is just the way it is. After all, you are two different people with two different spirits and personalities. We all like to be comfortable. When our wife does everything the way we like, we feel comfortable. When she does things differently than we like, that can make us uncomfortable. Just remember, each time you are uncomfortable with her actions or words, she may be equally as uncomfortable with yours, so try always to see life through her eyes. Seek to understand rather than to be understood. If you and your spouse each seek to understand each other instead of seeking to always be understood, life will be much more peaceful and fulfilling.

So, when considering a marriage partner, it is worth the effort to know yourself well enough to recognize what is important to you – discerning between things that will be a constant aggravation to you and things that will be minor irritations you can overlook and live with. Don't marry thinking you will fix all the things you don't like in your wife's personality – it won't happen.

What is important to you? What are important spousal qualities?

Consider things important to you that you are unwilling to sacrifice after marriage. This could include hobbies, religion, and friends. Whoever you choose as a partner should be compatible with who you are and willing to accept the things you are not willing to forfeit or you may have many struggles. For example, if you like to stay home but she wants to go out every night; that will be a problem. If you are a devoted Christian and she is not; that will likely be a problem. You must know yourself before you are ready to pick a partner for life.

After carefully considering your needs and wants, consider the qualities you desire in a spouse. The tendency for couples is to be on their best behavior when dating because they want to please each other. This may be consciously controlled behavior or subconsciously. It is natural to be on our best behavior when dating or considering marriage. That behavior should continue into marriage. Therefore, to prevent surprises after marriage, I encourage you to understand yourself and your future wife as well as possible before making that decision.

To get as true an understanding of your potential wife as possible, watch how she interacts with other people on a daily basis. Observe who she chooses as friends. Consider her conversations with others. Does she tend to speak positively or negatively about other people? Does she like to gossip? Does she tend to be self-centered and talk predominantly about herself or is she more interested in other people? Does she tend to be moody or is she consistently self-controlled. By observing how she treats other people, the things she likes to do, and the friends she chooses, you will gain insight into her true character and personality.

Now, I would like you to develop some lists to assist you gaining insight into your own personality and nature. This will help you understand what type of helpmate would be good for you and who you would be good for. These categories should stimulate your thinking to perhaps add more categories. Before you start, pray that God would open your understanding in this area so you get a true and accurate picture of yourself and what is important to you in marriage.

This is not meant to be, nor is it, a professionally developed profile exercise. I would recommend more detailed compatibility profiles for you and your prospective wife through pre-marital counseling service for a more complete understanding before making the marriage commitment. This exercise is simply to assist you in that process.

Qualities and characteristics I am looking for in a wife
1.
2.
3.
4.
5.

Activities and friends I enjoy and will not sacrifice after marriage.
1.
2.
3.
4.
5.

Activities and interests I would like my spouse to have in common with me to share time doing
1.
2.
3.
4.
5.

Habits and qualities I would find unacceptable in a wife.
1.
2.
3.
4.
5.

It would be advisable to revisit your lists periodically before marrying to ensure you are traveling down the road with the right one and as a refresher to understand where you are at any point in time. Because of experiences and maturing, you may find your lists changing over time. As you seek God and His guidance, you will discover your purposes in life more completely. As you understand God's calling on your life more fully, that will undoubtedly influence your decision in a helpmate.

Now I would like to briefly address a few things that may potentially cause conflict in a marriage relationship. This is by no means an all-inclusive list, but I include it to provide guidance and insight.

Potential sources of conflict in marriage

Sex-sex-sex. Sex is likely the major motivator for seeking marriage. We can enjoy meaningful and fulfilling friendships and companionship outside marriage, so sex is usually an important driving factor in considering marriage. So what does God's Word tell us about sex and marriage?

<u>1 Corinthians 7:1-5 (NIV – *emphasis added*)</u>
"Now for the matters you wrote about: It is good for a man not to marry. But since there is so much immorality, each man should have his own wife, and each woman her own husband. The husband should fulfill his marital duty to his wife, and likewise the wife to her husband. The wife's body does not belong to her alone but also to her husband. In the same way, the husband's body does not belong to him alone but also to his wife. Do not deprive each other except by mutual consent and for a time, so that you may devote yourselves to prayer. Then come together again so that Satan will not tempt you because of your lack of self-control."

Most of us seem to struggle with sex in one way or another. Natural sexual drive and lust can drive people to have sex before marriage, indulge infidelity within marriage, become addicted to pornography, and the list goes on. It seems there are an infinite number of ways to violate God's intended use for sex, which is to procreate and grow a married couple closer together through shared sexual enjoyment with each other. Study your wife to see what pleases her and let her know what pleases you so you can develop the most satisfying sexual relationship possible. The enjoyment of sex is one of our greatest gifts from God that He has given us, but it is meant to be enjoyed within the married relationship. You don't have to look far to see the devastating effects of sex outside of marriage.

Using sex to attract the opposite sex can lead people, especially young girls and women, to dress and act lewdly. Lack of self-control over sexual impulses can lead people into unhealthy sexual behaviors and relationships that cause great emotional damage. Many times, physical damage also occurs through sexually transmitted diseases. God purposed sex to be enjoyed between a husband and wife within the marriage relationship – period!

Sexual immorality is a common problem because the desire for sex is a strong impulse within most people and too many people choose not to exercise self-control over that impulse. And as you indulge that impulse, it becomes stronger, making it more difficult to control, as with any addiction. By definition, an addiction is simply an urge or habit that you surrender control to. The longer you indulge any habit or behavior, the more control the behavior has over you and the less control you have over it.

Another possible conflict in marriage is your faith. The importance of one's faith seems underestimated by many, if not most, people, in my opinion. When I was a teenager and started dating, my mother advised me to pick someone who believed as I did, which at that time meant someone attending a church of the same Christian denomination. With the smorgasbord of religions and unbelief in our world today, that advice takes on a whole new meaning. I have discovered that teaming up with a spouse having the same belief system is vitally important to harmony in marriage.

Our beliefs define us. Our beliefs determine how we view life and live life. I believe few people consider the importance of their faith in selecting their spouse. Many falsely assume their wife will go to their church or assume they will easily find a neutral church after marriage. I highly recommend that you choose a partner that believes as you do or you may experience more adversity than you currently foresee. Don't assume your wife will automatically go to your church. Many times, the man ends up going to his wife's church. Either that or they compromise and find an entirely new and different church that is neutral, but that may leave them both feeling dissatisfied. So seriously consider your faith and how your future wife's beliefs align with yours.

Children are another possible source of conflict. Some people love children and look forward to raising a large family, while others don't want children. And I don't believe I have ever met any two couples who agreed completely on how to raise or discipline children, so you must be ready to handle those differences in a mature way. I advise you to probe ahead of time to determine your future spouse's preference concerning children.

It may sound silly, but that goes for pets, too. If you love animals, you may not want to marry a person who hates animals. These are important things to discover before marriage. If you are already married, you have either worked through these differences or begun an emotional separation due to your differences. If the latter is the case, I again encourage you to seek marriage counseling to resolve your differences and find a solution so you can continue to enjoy and grow in your marriage.

The way Mom and Dad did it may be the cause of some of your initial petty arguments. Like I mentioned earlier, we like to feel comfortable. It's amazing what young married couples will find to argue about. Couples argue about how to wash dishes, how to fold towels properly, how to dress for certain occasions, how to celebrate certain occasions, and much more. Most of these arguments happen because we have grown up in different homes with different customs. There are seldom right or wrong ways to do many of the things we argue about; there are simply different ways of achieving the same outcome. Mostly, we like to keep doing things the same old way because it is comfortable. I simply bring this to your attention so you can work through that initial adaptation process more smoothly.

No matter how much you love your wife and she loves you, there will be a transition period in which you figure out your own system for doing things. During that transition, avoid taking those little unimportant things too seriously. You will find over time that most arguments are about trivial things not important enough to waste breath discussing. Usually at the root of every argument is pride – simply wanting to have your way because you want to have your way.

Here again, if you can't seem to maturely resolve your problems on your own, seek professional counseling from a Christian marriage counselor with a good reputation. As in any profession, there is a range of quality in counseling services, so be purposeful in seeking counseling based on recommendations from trusted friends and professionals. Then make sure you feel comfortable with your chosen counselor because you may be directed to a good counselor with a personality that conflicts with yours. A conflicting personality could minimize the effectiveness of your counseling. Therefore, if you don't feel comfortable with your initial visit, don't be afraid to seek a different counselor. When considering a counselor, a secular counselor may give some good behavioral advice and tools to improve your relationships, but they may lack the Christian worldview that will lead you to healing you need through Christ. So a good place to start is usually your own pastor.

Now we come to one of the biggest sources of conflicts in marriage – money. How to spend the money and how to raise the children are typically two of the strongest areas of contention in a marriage. When it comes to finances, the best advice I can give you is to keep God first in your life by tithing. Then live debt free as much as possible. God is more than able to meet your needs, and I have experienced that He is very willing to do so when we seek Him with our whole heart, mind, soul, and strength, remembering to keep Him first in our lives. Live responsibly and set right priorities for spending to experience financial prosperity to the fullest. I will discuss this in detail in Chapter 4.

When the honeymoon is over

After marriage, there seems to be a tendency to start being more concerned with our needs being met and less concerned with meeting our spouse's needs. I believe this partially results from the fact that as we begin forming lives together, we have bad moments when we are tired, abnormally stressed for one reason or another, or experience simply selfish moments when we just want our own way, moments when we blurt out something that causes hurt. Over time, as those moments add up, it can cause us to begin seeing our wife as an enemy rather than the friend she is intended to be. Through hurt, and our desire for comfort, we may begin building walls of protection, which is just another way of saying we begin turning off our affectionate feelings toward our wife to protect ourselves from further emotional hurt. This can lead to further isolation, withdrawal, and seeking happiness through means other than our spouse such as through hobbies, developing other friendships, over indulging in work, and etcetera.

Also, as we mature in our marriage relationship and become more familiar and comfortable with our spouse, there can be a tendency to start taking each other for granted. That is when those little things can become irritating because we have dealt with the big things. There seems to be a subconscious area of our brain that falsely concludes we have them now, so we can let up on our self-control and let our moods hang out, trusting our spouse to forgive us when we act badly.

Without the power of the Holy Spirit dwelling in us, it is nearly if not impossible to consistently feel love toward anyone. We are selfish by nature and doomed to failure without the power source dwelling in us. Even with the Holy Spirit's power and guidance, we will still have failing moments, but that is when we must trust the Holy Spirit in our spouse to work the grace of forgiveness so we can start afresh. A healthy marriage with the Holy Spirit is difficult enough. A healthy marriage without the Holy Spirit is nearly impossible in my opinion.

As you mature your marriage relationship, make a real effort to keep the honeymoon alive. Seek to discover new ways of ministering to your wife as you seek to continue maturing your relationship to her and God. Throughout your marriage, if you continue putting the same effort into your relationship as when you were dating, I don't believe the honeymoon need ever end. It may change as you mature the relationship, but it never need lose the pizzazz.

Married couples should never take each other for granted because they are a gift to each other from God and should value and appreciate each other as gifts from God. Marriage is a union intended to elevate the husband and wife above what they would be alone. Marriages grow stronger and more fulfilling when husbands and wives purpose to support, encourage, and love each other as they love themselves. Marriage is a gift from God to be cherished and nourished constantly.

Life-long commitment

Marriage is a life-long commitment that should be carefully thought through and talked through before the commitment. Marriage can be your most rewarding relationship or your worst nightmare if you choose the wrong spouse for the wrong reasons without giving your choice careful consideration and prayer.

As I stated in Chapter 1, my first marriage ended after twenty-six years, three hundred and thirty days. From the outset, I never considered divorce to be an option. When I married, I made a lifelong commitment. I never in my wildest dreams thought our marriage would end in divorce. But as I alluded to earlier, I think it was many little hurts and disappointments over many years that were never properly dealt with until we reached a point where we were both so focused on our own hurt we lost hope and gave up. I do know our divorce hurt our children in ways I will never fully comprehend because we can never truly put ourselves in someone else and experience their pain in the same way they do. Our divorce also took something out of me that will never be quite the same again. It is an experience I do not wish on anyone.

So if you are single, carefully consider who God has created you to be. We are all unique creations with certain wants, needs, and desires. Seek God's guidance to understand yourself and pray for God to direct you to the one He has created for you to spend your life with, if you were created to marry. Some are created without the need or desire for sex or the marriage relationship so they can devote their life to serving the Lord in ministry through their local church or serving their communities at large in some specific ways. Seek wisdom from the Lord. Ask Him to reveal to your calling and purpose in life so you follow your prepared path that results in a peaceful and content life.

If you are married, study the Scriptures to understand what a marriage relationship is meant to be so your marriage can grow healthy and strong through the Lord Jesus Christ who provides all good things to enjoy. Allow Christ to be the center of your life, if He is not already, so you can enjoy the inner peace and contentment that only He can provide. Seek to be the best husband you can be so your marriage relationship will continue to grow stronger as you enjoy the relationship the Lord blesses and sanctifies. Seek the welfare of your wife above your own. View her as the fragile, expensive, rare gift that she is. Learn to be tenderhearted – this is not natural for men, but essential to a good marriage relationship.

A wife's influence

This is especially important for the single men who are considering marriage. In Genesis 3:1-7, we read that Satan tempted the woman Eve to eat of the fruit of the Tree of the Knowledge of Good and Evil, tempting her with the ability to be like God. Eating the fruit, and even disobedience, weren't at the root of the fall of man – it was pride! Pride made the woman want to be like God. Then, having been deceived, she turned to her husband Adam, offering him the same temptation and he willingly rebelled against God.

God created Satan a powerful and beautiful angel in Heaven, but he was cast out when pride was found in him. In the process, he deceived a third of the angels in Heaven to follow him in his rebellion against God. Now he is running throughout the earth, attempting to deceive the human population into thinking they, too, can be their own god, thereby throwing away their salvation, peace, and Godly blessings. This is why we need to choose a Godly helpmate to help us maintain a Godly path. Let me explain.

In the beginning, in the Garden of Eden, it was the woman who was seduced by the attractiveness of the fruit and thought of becoming like God. She then offered the temptation to Adam and he ate of it. There is no inference that he resisted the temptation in any way. He willingly followed his wife's example and advice.

Other places in Scripture reveal that the wisest man who ever lived, King Solomon, ended his life in despair and felt all life was vanity because he had a woman problem. Solomon had made alliances with many heathen nations by marrying daughters of kings of those nations who worshipped other gods – all of them vile. Over time, his hundreds of wives and concubines influenced him to build temples to their gods throughout the nation of Israel, and Solomon began worshipping them himself. And as you would expect, after he turned away from God, he felt the despair and disappointment that naturally comes with abandoning God.

Women heavily influence men's decisions and direction in life. Most men will do whatever their wife wants because they love them and want to make them happy and avoid conflict. If you marry an ungodly woman, I can virtually guarantee she will have an ungodly influence on you. If you marry a Godly woman, she will have a Godly influence on you. Therefore, it is essential for your own well-being to choose the Godly wife prepared for you by your heavenly Father.

God created woman to be a helpmate, friend, companion, and partner in life to make man better than he would be on his own. Without women as nurturing and guiding influences, I am convinced man would have destroyed himself long before now. It is usually women who are trying to mend fences, nurture, and bring unity to relationships. Men more often tend to want to control everything and dominate over things. We need the two natures of men and women working together in unity to produce a Godly world, but we need to be joined with our match made in Heaven to fully realize the prosperous marriage we all want and hope for.

The marriage journey

I have come to realize as I write this book that life and marriage will never reach the perfect blissful plateau we all hope for and remain there. We live in a fallen world where things beyond our control happen every day – some good and some not so good. The fact that things are continually changing means we must continually adapt to change. Failing to adapt and deal with ongoing change results in disappointment and bitterness. The only way to maintain our peace and contentment is by acknowledging and accepting the fact change is inevitable. We have little control over our environment, people we come in contact with, or our wife's choices, so all we can do is work at responding correctly (Godly) to each situation.

God has given us control over only one person and that person is us. Part of the fruit of God's Spirit is self-control – not others-control. We are powerless to control others to always behave the way we want so we can remain perpetually comfortable. The best we can do is pray God will give us wisdom, clarity of mind and heart, and self-control to respond Godly to the negative circumstances and unfair treatment that will occur in our lives on perhaps a daily basis so we can maintain the peace He died to give us. We need to respond correctly to the positive things in our lives also, remembering to credit God for our blessings with thankful and grateful hearts.

So, as we discussed earlier, make every effort to shed your pride. Have mercy and show grace to yourself and your wife. Develop realistic expectations; no two people are the same and marriage requires constant adjustment. Every day, we make decisions big and small. Each of those decisions has the potential to change the course of our lives – affecting our wife and others in some way. Decisions we make might cause our wife offense in which case open communication, mercy, and grace are necessary to resolve the conflict. Without communication, misunderstandings and resentments may easily develop. Problems seldom solve themselves – they do not just go away. Without communication, problems do not get resolved.

Making decisions that affect your wife should be discussed with her before making them to avoid misunderstandings or conflict. Realize that you will likely never arrive at the fairy tale perfect marriage where you are perpetually happy every moment of every day. Life is a journey full of daily decisions that sometimes cause disappointment to you and your wife. Life is full of joys, disappointments, compromises, and adjustments that require forgiveness, mercy, and grace if you are going to experience joy and happiness on a continual basis.

Accept the fact that life consists of ups and downs and level ground and none of them are permanent – you will go through ups, downs, and walking on level ground throughout your life. You won't always like everything you do, and you won't always like everything your wife does. You need patience, love, forgiveness, grace, communication. For a healthy relationship, you need to consider the needs and happiness of your wife in everything you do.

Your wife is a precious gift from God. Treat her that way to experience the fullness of joy in the marriage relationship God initiated for your benefit. As I have already stated, God tells us to love our wife unconditionally as He loves us. Unconditional love is only possible for God, but as we mature in our relationship to God, our wife, and our fellow man, we should be increasingly reflecting that unconditional love in the way we live our lives. Surrender to that power source daily and enjoy the blessings that accompany that surrender.

May God bless you in your journey!

Chapter 4

Achieving spiritual and financial prosperity

The abundant life

*M*oney is important to everyone because we require it to trade for nearly everything we need and want in life. The good news is God wants to supply our every need and the Godly desires of our heart. For Him to accomplish that requires us having a Godly perspective and use of money. As we gain that Godly perspective, and respective use of our money, we also gain increasing spiritual prosperity.

John 10:10-11 (NKJV – *emphasis added*)
"The thief does not come except to steal and to kill and to destroy. I have come that they may have life and that they may have it more abundantly. I am the good Shepherd. The good Shepherd gives His life for the sheep."

Christ clearly stated the devil comes to steal the abundant life He died to give us. Christ died to make possible for us a joyful, fulfilled, and abundant life on this earth as well as eternally in Heaven. To realize what He died to provide for us, we look to Webster's Dictionary.

Abundant
Fully sufficient: every spiritual, emotional, and physical need is met
Richly supplied: God richly gives us all things to enjoy
Rarely in want: even though we may temporarily be in want of some thing, remember that it is temporary
Jesus came to give us full sufficiency in all things – lacking no good thing. That means God wills that you experience abundance in physical, emotional, mental, and financial health.

To enjoy that abundant life, there are key things for you to realize. The first is that God requires you to love mercy (be forgiving), do justly, and walk humbly with Him, seeking His kingdom and His righteousness above everything else as we discovered in Chapter 2.

WARNING! Prosperity may be dangerous to your health

Before leading you through the pathway to prosperity, I want to warn you as God warned the Israelites before they passed into the Promised Land of the dangers of becoming financially prosperous.

Before they ever entered the Promised Land, God warned the Jewish nation through Moses that after He had prospered them, they would forget about Him and go chasing after other gods to worship. The only viable explanation I can conceive for this is they would turn away from God through pride. Pride causes us to believe we are accumulating everything God gives us through our own intellect, talents, and abilities. We so easily forget the source of our ability to accumulate wealth.

History has shown us repeatedly that as nations increase in prosperity, they eventually peak and then begin to decline – sometimes quickly, sometimes slowly. I once heard a quote that has stuck with me. Someone in our past said "No nation has ever survived prosperity." This may seem difficult to understand, so let me explain what the Lord has revealed to me concerning this phenomenon.

Recently, the Lord showed me how nations throughout history have pridefully gone from nation conquering to build and expand their empires only to eventually retreat to where they began, often to an even smaller area than they originally enjoyed and with less national power. As with the nation of Israel, it has become obvious to me that God has allotted to every individual and nation a defined area and space. Individuals as well as nations will often take away from others to accumulate more for them when given the opportunity.

Through pride and arrogance, many men and nations throughout history have gone about seeking to take away from others what does not belong to them. This kingdom building succeeds for a time – sometimes hundreds of years – but eventually the oppressed are delivered through one source or another by God when they cry out to Him for help. God says He hears the cries of those who are downtrodden and oppressed, and He does not allow that to go on forever. The key here is turning to God – Jesus – Father, Son, and Holy Ghost. Many people and nations live in constant oppression and torment because they seek relief through worthless gods and religions that have no power to help them, or they try delivering themselves through their own power and intelligence. There is only one God and His redeeming name is Jesus. Those who call upon the name of the Lord Jesus will be saved from their sins and their enemies, and they will experience prosperity in body, soul, and spirit.

Another danger of prosperity is the damage it can bring to relationships. We are all born selfish through the original sin inherited because of Adam and Eve's rebellion against God. Operating through an unregenerate selfish nature, we struggle to meet our basic needs by forming bonds with our wife, children, neighbors, and others in our society to survive and get what we want. In this unregenerate state, we are not being kind and cooperative out of a bond of love, but out of need. As unregenerate people become more prosperous and need others less, I have seen their relationships begin to sever except for the ones they truly value and want to maintain. Here again, they maintain those relationships basically out of selfishness, not love.

One example of this prosperity phenomenon was demonstrated through a couple who won a large lottery years ago. I heard of a young couple who planned to marry. After winning the multi-million dollar lottery, they apparently decided to call off the marriage and go off to enjoy their money alone. How their story is progressing I don't know, but I know that without a Godly perspective on money and a strong relationship with Jesus, money has a strong tendency to entice us into many unhealthy behaviors.

I have not followed any of the lives of people who have come by wealth quickly, but through cases made aware through public media, there is seldom a good outcome to instant wealth. Not only is this obvious through those who win large amounts of money through gambling, but it has also been made obvious through the stories of a number of young professional athletes who receive millions of dollars in wages to play professional sports and proceed to ruin their lives through immoral living or unwisely squandering all of their income in a short amount of time only to end in poverty at the end of their often short careers.

God has much to say about money in the Holy Bible, and when it comes to get rich quick schemes, He says He hates them. Anyone looking to get rich quick through gambling or risky investments demonstrates a love of money and therefore cannot love God. Jesus confirmed this when He said you can't love and serve both. Jesus said you will love and serve God or you will love and serve money. You can't do both.

Matthew 6: 24 (NKJV – *emphasis added*)
"No one can serve two masters; for either he will hate the one and love the other or else he will be loyal to the one and despise the other. You cannot serve God and mammon (wealth)."

So, I caution you. After God has prospered you, do not forget Him! Keep your focus on God and you will be able to enjoy a long, prosperous, and content life.

Keeping your focus on God's kingdom and His righteousness

In the sixth chapter of Matthew's gospel, Jesus talks about this principle, making it clear God has no problem with you having wealth and things to enjoy, but He insists you first focus on seeking His kingdom and doing right with your whole heart, mind, soul, and strength first – not seeking to fulfill your own selfish desires.

If you focus on money, you may get it, but you will also experience the curses of worry, anxiety, fatigue, and stress that accompany that focus. If you focus on God, you will find that you are increasingly enjoying inner peace and contentment as God brings to you the desires of your heart through a variety of ways. Patiently walking the Godly path results in God prospering you without sorrows added.

After warning about the love of money, Jesus went on to tell the disciples not to worry about getting money (implied), clothes, food, or other things the world seeks after, pointing out that God the Father took care of everything in nature, so He would certainly take care of them if they would just keep their focus on Him, trust Him, and continually seek to do His will.

Matthew 6:33-34 (NKJV – *emphasis added*)
"But seek first the kingdom of God and His righteousness, and all these things shall be added to you. Therefore do not worry about tomorrow, for tomorrow will worry about its own things. Sufficient for the day is its own trouble."

James 4:2-4 (NKJV – *emphasis added*)
"You lust and do not have. You murder and covet and cannot obtain. You fight and war. Yet you do not have because you do not ask. You ask and do not receive because you ask amiss, that you may spend it on your pleasures. Adulterers and adulteresses! Do you not know that friendship with the world is enmity with God? Whoever therefore wants to be a friend of the world makes himself an enemy of God."

When you surrender your life and will into God's hands, He begins "giving" you the good desires of your heart without you seeking them, and Scripture reveals there is no sorrow or anxiety accompanying God's blessings.

Now, understand that I am not saying you don't have to work for those things. You cannot sit in an easy chair with remote control in hand, expecting God to drop everything you need and want into your lap. He is a God that expects you to work. We read in the Bible that anyone who won't work won't eat. What it means is that as you seek to get closer to God, He will direct your path toward prosperity in every way so you can have sufficiency in all things to overflowing. Then you will be equipped spiritually, emotionally, and financially to share and bless others' lives as well. He will bring people and opportunities into your life to prosper you financially, emotionally, and spiritually. He will prosper your soul and spirit as you continually seek Him through prayer and His Word, the Holy Bible, and go about doing good deeds for others. As you increasingly get your focus off money and yourself – focusing on the needs of others instead – you will find yourself feeling more joy, peace, and contentment as you increasingly experience God's blessings in your life.

God the Father is a generous God. In return for His love and generosity and rewards, He desires your love, devotion, and obedience. Yes, God does reward us for good motives and behavior. That might sound contrary to many Christian teachings, but the Bible says it is impossible to please God if you don't believe He will reward you.

Hebrews 11:6 (NKJV – *emphasis added*)
"But without faith it is impossible to please Him, for he who comes to God must believe that He is, and that He is a rewarder of those who diligently seek Him."

God longs to be compassionate and kind to us, but it is a two way street, and He expects some effort on our part in the relationship. Our part is to seek to know Him better and be thankful and grateful for all He has done and continues to do for us.

Tithing and its importance in receiving God's blessings

The beginning of wisdom in financial responsibility and prosperity begins with tithing. A major key to seeing your needs met and desires fulfilled starts with tithing. The first ten percent of your earnings belong to God. If you refuse to tithe, you are robbing God, as revealed through the prophet Malachi. I recognized this truth when studying God's Word nearly thirty-five years ago. At that time, I began tithing because I recognized it was the right thing to do. As I faithfully brought my tithes to church, God supplied all of my needs. Since then, as I have gone considerably beyond the tithe with liberality in offerings and helping others, God has increased His blessings in my life so I can be even more generous. As I said, God is a generous God and wants us to be generous. I have experienced this principle firsthand and can attest to God's faithfulness to increase your prosperity as you increase your generosity in spreading the gospel and helping those in need.

God reveals the reason for tithing in Deuteronomy 14:23 through Moses when He said tithing is meant to remind us to keep God first in our life. It then goes on to say tithes and offerings brought into His storehouse (your local church) are meant to pay the clergy and take care of widows, orphans, and foreigners living among us. So tithe because it is the right thing to do. Don't tithe because you want to make a bargain with God to make you rich. Remember that *God looks into your heart to see your motives*. Don't think you can outsmart God. You may be able to fool people with your outward actions, but God looks at your heart to see why you do what you do. Therefore, if you tithe with right motives, you can expect God to take care of every one of your needs while you rest in His love. If you tithe with wrong motives to make a bargain for gain from God, you will find yourself dissatisfied and likely full of anxiety and bitterness because your perverted motives will result in frustrated expectations.

God's purpose in prospering you abundantly

God does not provide abundant wealth and resources strictly for our own selfish consumption, as we read in the fourth chapter of James; even though He certainly does give us richly all things to enjoy. In 2 Corinthians 9:6-12, the apostle Paul summarizes well God's main reason for blessing us with overflowing abundance. There are other Scriptures that confirm this truth.

2 Corinthians 2:6-12 (NKJV – *emphasis added*)
*"But this I say: 'He who sows sparingly will also reap sparingly, and he who sows bountifully will also reap bountifully. So let each one give as he purposes in his heart, not grudgingly or of necessity; for **God loves a cheerful giver**. And **God is able to make all grace abound toward you that you always having all sufficiency in all things may have an abundance for every good work**. As it is written:*

'He has dispersed abroad.
He has given to the poor;
His righteousness endures forever.'

*Now may He who supplies seed to the sower, and bread for food, supply and multiply the seed you have sown and increase the fruits of your righteousness, **while you are enriched in everything for all liberality, which causes thanksgiving through us to God**.*

There are several important keys to take away from those verses. First, you must remember, as we already covered, tithing (giving the first ten percent of your income) is not giving or sowing – it is more like dues owed. This is made clear through other Scripture verses that we won't go into here – both from the Old Testament and New Testament. To reiterate, God revealed through the prophet Malachi that if you do not bring your tithe into the storehouse (the church you are a member of), you are robbing Him. So when we talk of sowing bountifully, we are referring to money we give over and above the tithe – our excess.

If you expect God to generously bless you beyond your basic needs, then be a cheerful giver who sows into the needs of peoples' lives. You sow into peoples' lives by sowing money to see the Word of God – the Good News – spread throughout the world, as well as supplying provision for their physical and emotional well-being. Your gifts of money cause the Word of God to spread and provide for the needs of the poor, orphans, widows, foreigners, and the hungry, causing them to praise God and give Him glory. The way you live your life and the deeds and words you minister to others are also ways of sowing the seed of the Word. Financially, however, I have experienced that the more you give, the more God gives back to you so that you can be even more generous. When you finally get a Godly perspective on money and quit trusting in it, God seems to open up His wallet because He knows you will use your money in a Godly manner, not just consuming it on yourself.

I am not insinuating, however; nor am I recommending, you give all your money away in the hopes God will double it back to you. Tithing is a requirement and reveals the condition of your heart and thinking toward God. Giving beyond the tithe is done with wisdom from a willing and generous heart as God prospers you. God is not asking you to take food out of your family's mouth to give to others, but as He prospers you, He is looking for you to be conscious of the needs of those around you and provide for their needs as you are able. When you do, you will find God increasingly blessing you spiritually, emotionally, and financially. God's best blessings are spiritual, but He knows you need material things to live and enjoy also, so those are thrown in as you keep a proper outward focus and perspective on money.

So if you have found yourself always lacking money to supply your needs, I recommend you examine your priorities. Look at your checkbook and see where all your money goes. How much is going to the church and taking care of others' needs versus what you spend for your own enjoyments and entertainment.

God's will for your life

Since blessings come through seeking God's kingdom and doing what is right, we need to know what that entails. We find the answers throughout the Bible, but there are a couple especially good summary passages to check your spiritual maturity level and level of obedience to the will of God. The first is found in the book of Galatians.

Galatians 5:22-26 (NKJV – *emphasis added*)
But the fruit of the Spirit is love (charity), joy, peace, longsuffering (patience), kindness, goodness, faithfulness, gentleness, self-control; *against such there is no law. And those who are Christ's have crucified the flesh with its passions and desires. If we live in the Spirit, let us also walk in the Spirit. Let us not become conceited, provoking one another, envying one another."*

And:

Micah 6:8 (NKJV – *emphasis added*)
*"He (God) has shown you, O man, what is good; and **what does the Lord require of you**, but to **do justly, love mercy, and to walk humbly with your God."***

Another check on your spiritual maturity is found in 1 Corinthians chapter 13 – the "Love Chapter." This chapter summarizes what Godly love is and is not like. The apostle Paul beautifully summarizes the importance of living a life of love above all other things. I encourage you to take time to read it in your Bible now and read it often to remind yourself what God's perfect love, will, and nature look like. God's general will for your life is that you emulate His image. 1 Corinthians 13 well summarizes that image.

Pride – the wall blocking God's favor

Even though we dealt with pride in Chapter 2, it is so important I want to revisit it here briefly. Pride is a wall between you and God that prevents God's blessings from flowing into your life.

All humanity struggles with pride, some of us more than others. We all must humble ourselves if we want to advance in God's kingdom and receive His bountiful blessings. I'm including here just a few verses from the Bible dealing with the evils of pride. I encourage you to do a search of your own to more fully understand the devastating effects of pride. Refer back to Chapter 2 for definitions relating to pride.

Proverbs 13:10 (NJKV *– emphasis added*)
"By pride comes nothing but strife, but with the well-advised is wisdom."

Proverbs 16:18-19 (NJKV *– emphasis added*)
"Pride goes before destruction and a haughty spirit before a fall. Better to be of a humble spirit with the lowly, than to divide the spoil with the proud."

As you can see, our pride leads us to our own destruction. It is not a matter of if it will destroy us, it is only a matter of time before we bring about our own demise if we do not humble ourselves before God and do what is right and good. The destruction may be a slow, emotionally painful life caused by bitterness over unmet expectations. Or the destruction may be a sudden disaster caused by cheating or lying in some form. Regardless, pride leads to discontentment, bitterness, anxiety, and every other evil.

1 Peter 5:5b-9 (NJKV *– emphasis added*)
*"...all of you be submissive to one another, and be clothed with humility, for '**God resists the proud, but gives grace to the humble**.' Therefore humble yourselves under the mighty hand of God that He may exalt you in due time; casting all your care upon Him, for He cares for you. Be sober (clear thinking); be vigilant; because your adversary the devil walks about like a roaring lion seeking whom he may devour. Resist him steadfast in the faith, knowing that the same sufferings are experienced by your brotherhood in the world."*

Here are a few examples of how pride behaves.

Signs of pride:
Belittling other men's ideas.
Pointing out how you did something better than someone else.
Always seeking to have more just to build your ego and feel you are better than others.
Driving the right car or having the right house to feel important.
Disregarding your wife's needs to do what you want to do.
Feeling offended whenever your opinion is not accepted

Exulting yourself for your accomplishments rather than giving God the glory for giving you your talents and abilities.
Judging others' actions by your own sense of goodness.

Gossiping about another. Gossip is one way of bringing another person down to cause you to feel elevated in your own mind over them.

Those are just a few examples to help you realize how prideful human nature is.

Husband and wife – working in unity
(for married couples or those considering marriage)

To be individually and jointly prosperous in finances, spirit, soul, and body, husbands and wives must be working together in unity, loving each other as the Bible instructs.

I have yet to meet any two married couples who run their finances and checkbook exactly the same way. How to run finances within a marriage is something that each couple must work out for themselves – with a Christian financial advisor's help if necessary.

I also know that people are only too willing to tell you how you should do it. My advice is to work out a system with your wife that the two of you feel comfortable with. This may take time as you tweak your system to arrive at one you both feel comfortable with. Since money is such an important issue in "all" marriages and to each of us individually, it is important to eliminate this area of possible contention by agreeing on a system – even if you need professional help to do it. Certainly seek advice from others who are good money managers if you are having budgeting or spending issues, but take their advice and mold it into a system that works for you.

Budget your money – and stick to it

Many people find themselves in financial difficulty because they do not budget their money. To be financially responsible, you must budget your money. I discovered this reality after my first child was born and we bought a house. Before house and children, I wasn't too concerned about budgeting money and basically spent everything pretty carefree. Once the responsibilities started increasing, I found I needed to get serious with the money situation.

Here is the process I adopted that may benefit you. If not, I encourage you to develop your own budgeting system. Each month, I type a list of monthly bills and spending allowances and tape it in the back of my checkbook register. Then as I pay each bill, I cross it off the list. This enables me to know based on my income how much discretionary money I have left for the month. That is how I got a grip on my spending years ago and it has helped me immensely to stay on track and stay focused. Few things in life cause more stress than money issues – especially within marriage – so I encourage you to work out a budget to help keep your spending in check and priorities taken care of.

The next few pages contain sample budget outlines to help you in your budget planning, tables, and formulas to help you understand compound interest and loan repayments and an example monthly budgeting list similar to the one I put in my checkbook each month. Many of your monthly expenses should be pretty consistent, so in your checkbook, you may be able to list some of your expenses to the penny, which will help you with your budgeting as time goes on.

Living on a budget – sample table of expenses with comments

Budget Item	*Comments*
Church giving (tithing)	Biblically, tithing is a requirement for several reasons. Tithing with right motives, remembering to keep God the top priority in our lives, produces a blessing. Jesus talked much about money because the way we spend money reveals our priorities. To see where your priorities are, look in your checkbook
House Payment or Rent	Should not be more than twenty-five percent of your gross income. More than that will create a heavy financial burden.
Electricity	Usually a necessity.
Phone	Usually a necessity.
House Gas (Heat)	If you own a home, and depending on the climate you live in, an appropriate amount of attic insulation can be extremely important to keep down heating costs and save on air conditioning costs. The cost to insulate the attic can many times be easily recovered within very few years through savings in utility costs.
Water/Garbage/Sewer	Usually necessary if you own a home in a city.
Clothes	If on a restricted budget, there are several recycling and thrift stores with good clothes for low prices.
Savings/Investments	The earlier you can start saving, the faster your money grows. Company matching 401(K) pre-tax plans are currently the best investments going that I am aware of, so if your company offers one, take advantage of the pre-tax savings. If you cannot put in the maximum allowable by the IRS, at least put in as much as the company will match because it is free money.
Car Maintenance	Properly maintaining a car can save you money in the long run.
Credit Cards	Because of the extremely high interest rates, pay them off each month to avoid finance charges.
Car Payments	Only buy what you need, or falls easily into your budget.

Food	Avoid smoking, snacks, sodas and alcohol. Buy essentials and staple foods with good nutritious value.
House/Renters Insurance	Home owners insurance is typically a requirement when carrying a home mortgage.
Life Insurance	Not meant to be an investment, but gives peace of mind knowing you have money for loved ones to carry on if you die unexpectedly.
Doctors/Dentists/ Medications	Determine your average monthly expenses for budgeting purposes.
School expenses	Determine your average monthly expenses for budgeting purposes.
Car Insurance	Usually a requirement if you own a car. If you have a car loan, the bank will likely require you to carry full coverage auto insurance until the loan is paid off.
Help for low-income groups	Food stamps, income based housing, assistance for dependant children. Check with local government agencies for help.
Fun	Some recreation is necessary for a healthy and happy life, so budget some money for fun and relaxation if possible.
Other	Modify the list as necessary to include your normal expense items.

The effect of compound interest versus time
(See how your money grows)

You start investing at age 20

and you quit investing at age 40

Age	$ Investment per year	Account balance at 7% per year compound interest
20	$1000	$1000.00
21	$1000	$2072.51
22	$1000	$3222.78
23	$1000	$4456.46
24	$1000	$5779.59
25	$1000	$7198.66
26	$1000	$8720.62
27	$1000	$10,352.94
28	$1000	$12,103.61
29	$1000	$13,981.22
30	$1000	$15,994.97
31	$1000	$18,154.74
32	$1000	$20,471.10
33	$1000	$22,955.43
34	$1000	$25,619.88
35	$1000	$28,477.53
36	$1000	$31,542.39
37	$1000	$34,829.47
38	$1000	$38,354.89
39	$1000	$42,135.93
40	$1000	$46,191.13
41	0	$49,540.37
42	0	$53,132.45
43	0	$56,984.99

You start investing at age 40

And you quit investing at age 60

Age	$ Investment per year	Account balance at 7% per year compound interest
20	0	0
21	0	0
22	0	0
23	0	0
24	0	0
25	0	0
26	0	0
27	0	0
28	0	0
29	0	0
30	0	0
31	0	0
32	0	0
33	0	0
34	0	0
35	0	0
36	0	0
37	0	0
38	0	0
39	0	0
40	$1000	$1000.00
41	$1000	$2072.51
42	$1000	$3222.78
43	$1000	$4456.46

44	0	$61,116.87	44	$1000	$5779.59
45	0	$65,548.34	45	$1000	$7198.66
46	0	$70,301.13	46	$1000	$8720.62
47	0	$75,398.54	47	$1000	$10,352.94
48	0	$80,865.55	48	$1000	$12,103.61
49	0	$86,728.96	49	$1000	$13,981.22
50	0	$93,017.52	50	$1000	$15,994.97
51	0	$99,762.05	51	$1000	$18,154.74
52	0	$106,995.62	52	$1000	$20,471.10
53	0	$114,753.68	53	$1000	$22,955.43
54	0	$123,074.26	54	$1000	$25,619.88
55	0	$131,998.15	55	$1000	$28,477.53
56	0	$141,569.09	56	$1000	$31,542.39
57	0	$151,834.01	57	$1000	$34,829.47
58	0	$162,843.22	58	$1000	$38,354.89
59	0	$174,650.68	59	$1000	$42,135.93
60	**0**	**$187,314.29**	**60**	**$1000**	**$46,191.13**

Note: The calculations use a lump sum investment at the end of each year. Interest in the example is not accumulating during the year, so if the investments were periodically invested during the year, the balances would be greater than listed.

Monthly Budget Worksheet

Budget item	Amount – Plan 1	Amount – Plan 2	Amount – Plan 3
Church			
House Payment/Rent			
House/Renters Insurance			
Food			
Electricity			
Heat			
Internet service			
Phone			
Water/Garbage/Sewer			
Clothes			
Savings/Investments			
Car Payments			
Car Insurance			
Car Maintenance			
Credit Cards			
Life Insurance			
Doctor/Dentist/Meds			
School Expenses			
Fun			
Other			
Other			
Other			
Monthly Net Income	$	$	$
Total of Expenses from Budgeted Items	$	$	$
Monthly Net Income (minus) Budgeted expenses	$	$	$

Notes and helpful hints:
1. If expenses in the Plan 1 worksheet exceed your income, look for the areas where you can control expenses. Set priorities so you meet essential budget items first as you create your budget Plan 2. Follow this process until your expenses are less than your monthly income.
2. Do not carry more cash than you need for your outing to avoid emotional spontaneous spending.
3. If you struggle to resist spontaneous emotional spending, do not carry your credit card unless you are traveling or have an emergency need. This will help you resist emotional buying.

Monthly Payment Quick Reference Chart

	Monthly Payment per $1000 Borrowed						
Yearly Interest Rate	Loan term: 2 years (24 months)	Loan term: 3 years (36 months)	Loan term: 4 years (48 months)	Loan term: 5 years (60 months)	Loan term: 6 years (72 months)	Loan term: 15 years (180 months)	Loan term: 30 years (360 months)
4.5%	$43.65	$29.75	$22.80	$18.64	$15.87	$7.65	$5.07
5%	$43.87	$29.97	$23.03	$18.87	$16.10	$7.91	$5.37
5.5%	$44.10	$30.20	$23.26	$19.10	$16.34	$8.17	$5.68
6%	$44.32	$30.42	$23.49	$19.33	$16.57	$8.44	$6.00
6.5 %	$44.54	$30.64	$23.71	$19.56	$16.81	$8.71	$6.32
7%	$44.77	$30.87	$23.94	$19.80	$17.04	$8.98	$6.65
7.5%	$45.00	$31.10	$24.17	$20.03	$17.29	$9.27	$6.99
8%	$45.22	$31.33	$24.41	$20.27	$17.53	$9.55	$7.33
8.5%	$45.45	$31.56	$24.64	$20.51	$17.77	$9.84	$7.68
9%	$45.68	$31.80	$24.88	$20.75	$18.02	$10.14	$8.04
9.5%	$45.91	$32.03	$25.12	$21.00	$18.27	$10.44	$8.40
10%	$46.14	$32.26	$25.36	$21.24	$18.52	$10.74	$8.79
10.5%	$46.37	$32.50	$25.60	$21.49	$18.77	$11.05	$9.14

Example loan:
If you borrow $6000 for 5 years at an annual percentage interest rate of 8%:
1. Go to the row in the chart with a yearly interest rate of 8%
2. Go across to the column that relates to the loan term of 5 years (60 months).
3. The dollar amount in that box is $20.27.
4. You are borrowing $6000, so you multiply 6 times $20.27 to get your monthly payment
5. 6 x $20.27 = $121.62
6. In this example, your monthly payment would be $121.62 to borrow $6000 for 5 years (60 months) at an annual percentage interest rate of 8%.

Investment Compound Interest Earnings Calculation Example

This first example is for those hate math or do not use a scientific calculator.

For this example you will be:
-*Investing $1000*
-*Investing the money at an annual interest rate of 7%*
-*Investing the money for 20 years*

For this example: E = D times C
E = future money
D = today's money
C = A raised to the power of B

A = e (base of natural system of logarithms – its value is approximately 2.71828):
Therefore A = 2.71828

B = (annual interest rate percentage) times (the number of years the money is invested):
Therefore **B** = (7% divided by 100) times (20 years)
Therefore **B** = .07 times 20
Therefore B = 1.400

C = A raised to the power of B
Therefore **C** = 2.71828 raised to the power of 1.4
Therefore **C** = $2.71828^{1.4}$
Therefore C = 4.0552

D = $1000 (amount of initial investment money)

To determine what your invested money will be worth:
E = D times **C**
Therefore E = $1000 times 4.0552

And the final answer is:
E = $4055.20 = the amount of money you would have if you made a one-time investment of $1000 and left it in the investment for 20 years at an annual percentage rate of 7%

Compound Interest Rate Formula:

For those with scientific calculators and knowledge of such calculations using the same example:

Future money = Initial principle times e^{rt} = \$1000 times $e^{(.07 \times 20)}$ = \$4055.20

Where:

- $e =$ base of the natural system of logarithms
- $r =$ annual interest rate percentage
- $t =$ number of years the money is invested

Sample Checkbook Ledger
(Create a new one each month and tape it in your checkbook register)

January Checkbook Budget (assuming 4 weeks per month)

Church tithe and offerings weekly ($, $, $, $)	$ Monthly total
Other Donations weekly ($, $, $, $)	$ Monthly total
Savings acct ($, $, $, $)	$ Monthly total
Mortgage Payment (date due)	$ Monthly total
Car Payment (date due)	$ Monthly total
House Fuel (date due)	$ Monthly total
Phone (date due)	$ Monthly total
Life Insurance (date due)	$ Monthly total
Electricity (date due)	$ Monthly total
Car Insurance (date due)	$ Monthly total
Cable TV (date due)	$ Monthly total
Car Gas ($, $, $, $) – Four fill-ups per month	$ Monthly total
Cash ($, $, $, $)	$ Monthly total
Car Maintenance	$ Monthly total
School expenses:	$ Monthly total
Internet service (date due)	$ Monthly total
Medical expenses	$ Monthly total
Clothing expenses	$ Monthly total

Credit Card Charges

??	$
??	$
??	$
??	$

Fill in the actual due dates and $'s with actual budgeted dollar amounts for your situation and add or change items as they apply to you.

My financial story

I provided you in Chapter 1 a snapshot of my life's story and how, when I was in my twenties, I diligently sought comfort and strength through God's Word. I then revealed how that led to service and leadership within the church. Now I would like to reveal what the Lord showed me concerning tithing on that first reading through His Testimony, the Holy Bible, and how that has affected me financially.

I have found as I study God's Word that each time through, there seems to be one particular theme connecting throughout the Bible that the Lord wants to anchor in my spirit and soul. That first time through it was tithing. I had never been taught tithing in the church in which I grew up or the church I attended through much of my adult life. When money was discussed, it was usually anxiously along the lines of begging because bills weren't being paid or there was some special need. When giving was mentioned, it was almost apologetically and implied or explicitly stated that tithing was an Old Testament requirement for the Jewish people that no longer applies so we could feel comfortable giving whatever we want.

Well, I have found they were wrong. I have heard teaching on tithing the past few years – how it has always been and continues to be a requirement of God's, Old and New Testament alike. The teaching confirms what I have experienced. I have found God true to His Word concerning the blessings associated with tithing and generous giving.

After the Lord emphasized the theme of tithing to me, I began tithing because I understood it was the right thing to do. Having always wanted to do the right thing, I started tithing when I was in the worst financial condition of my life. I was a young married man with two young children, a small modest house we struggled to pay for, and increasing credit card debt because my income was inadequate to meet my family's basic needs.

Shortly after I started tithing, I approached the bank to increase our checking account line of credit so we could make it through the next few months just getting by on necessities. And back then, necessities were grocery store food (no eating out other than an occasional fast food meal), mortgage, utilities, children's clothes, doctor bills, and gas for the car. We had no cell phones, electronic games, computers, none of the modern so-called necessities that people have become accustomed to today. Money was in short supply and we made an honest effort to live within our means. We had made the decision that my wife would stay home to raise the kids, but at that time, if she had worked, it would have cost more for daycare than what she would have earned working. Neither of us had a college education and our income earning potential was limited.

The first few months were pretty tight. God didn't instantly drop a bag of money out of Heaven to meet our every need just because we were tithing. What did happen over the next two years, however, proved God's faithfulness as I remained faithful to tithe.

Within two years of initially tithing, I had received a promotion and two good raises at work. Over those two years, I was able to pay off the credit card debt, quit my second job, and actually put away a little money each month. Since then, I have never had a credit card charge I have not been able to pay off at the end of the month. I have had enough money to meet my family's needs and be increasingly generous in helping others. I was also able to help my children through college. I have since always had a good, running, dependable car, and the Lord has provided for several nice vacations. All that began with tithing. God promises to meet all of our needs when we tithe and keep our focus on Him and loving others.

Several years ago, a visiting bishop at our church talked about the increased blessings associated with generous giving above and beyond the tithe. I had wanted to increase my giving above tithing for years but hadn't quite worked up the courage to do it. God was meeting my needs with a little extra to enjoy and I wasn't sure I wanted to give up that extra money that I was enjoying for eating out periodically and buying a few luxury items. But something in me burst open with excitement as he spoke. I turned to my wife in church and said I wanted to double our giving. She said, "Go for it."

Since dramatically increasing my giving, God has brought increase into my life through raises, overtime, and bonuses so that I have never missed the extra money I began giving. In fact, I have experienced more free money to spend than I had before. There have also been a number of occasions when the Lord has directed me to give away thousands of dollars to individuals. Sometimes it really stretched my budget when He directed me to give it away. But, in a fairly short period of time, He had replaced that money with unexpected overtime, tax return, or year-end bonus – usually providing more than what I had given so I could continue to be generous. I have learned that part of the reason God will direct you to stretch your giving at times is so you learn to depend on Him fully and experience His faithfulness in providing for you as you are obedient to His voice.

The Bible reveals to us a generous God and Father, and He wants us to be generous children. God blesses faithfulness and generosity. As you are faithful to obey His command to love Him and one another, He will faithfully supply your every need. But it takes faith and perseverance. Our adversary, Satan, manipulates financial circumstances at times in our lives to test our faith to see if we really believe what we say we believe. You may be tempted to quit tithing at those moments, but I encourage you to persevere and continue tithing through the tough times. If you remain faithful, you will find God to be faithful.

Financial rewards are the least of God's blessings

Blessings you receive for faithfully tithing and generously giving are much more than money. Many of the best blessings are spiritual blessings of peace, joy, and contentment. God wants to generously supply you because He knows your needs, but He wants you to maintain a proper attitude toward it. The more you focus your attention on God and wean your mind from thinking about money, the more you will find God supplying you with more money to share and enjoy. But be patient. God's provision normally increases over time because instant wealth can be spiritually devastating.

Our main reason for wanting excess is usually to feel more secure, power, or pride, which means money has become a god. Depending on money always leaves you feeling anxious and insecure because you realize how quickly it can disappear. That insecurity caused by trusting in a false god causes constant worrying about how much you need and worrying if you will have enough for the future. When you learn to put your total trust in God, you will find that your bank balance does not determine your peace, contentment, or happiness because you know where your source is. God is your source – not the bank. If you can anchor that truth in your heart and ignore contrary messages from the world and Satan, you will never worry about or lack needed money.

So begin enjoying spiritual and financial prosperity today by keeping your focus on loving God with your whole heart, mind soul, and strength, loving others as much as you love yourself, and by being a generous giver – in time, love, and money.

Chapter 5

Raising children successfully

Our children did not ask to come into this world, and as such, they owe us nothing as their parents except obedience, honor, and respect. We, on the other hand, owe them the best upbringing we can give them.

<u>Ephesians 6:4 (NKJV – *emphasis added*)</u>
"...fathers, do not provoke your children to wrath, but bring them up in the training and admonition of the Lord."

To successfully raise children requires a healthy, God-centered marriage and personal relationship with God.

The importance of a Godly father role model

For proper development, children need a strong father who demonstrates the *fruit of God's Spirit – love (charity), joy, peace, patience (long-suffering), goodness, faithfulness, kindness, gentleness, and self-control*. We all have off moments when we obviously fail to emulate God's nature, but our consistent and predominant behavior should reflect that of Christ as demonstrated through the fruit produced.

As you no doubt have discovered in your own life, parents may offer good advice and set rules that are proper and good, but children often follow the example rather than the spoken word. If you smoke but tell your children not to smoke, they will likely smoke, too. If you use vulgar language but tell your children not to, they will likely use vulgar language, too. It has been said a picture is worth a thousand words – you are their picture.

We are all naturally selfish and self-centered to some degree. From my observations, a large percentage of the population will indulge unhealthy behaviors and lusts if a means to justify their behavior is available. For a child, their father is a perfect excuse – if Dad does it, then it must be okay for me to do. Even if they know in their heart it is wrong to do, they will likely do whatever misguided deeds are in their heart if they can justify them through their father's actions.

Since fathers are so important to their children's development, if you are a father, I encourage and urge you to seek God's guidance through reading His Word, connecting with Godly men within the church, going to marriage and child-rearing counseling, and whatever else you may need to grow and mature into the man God intends you to be. The man you need to be for your children to properly develop into mature men and women. It will take effort. Being a REAL man takes effort. That is why consciously counting the cost of marriage and fatherhood is important before traveling that path. *Marriage and being a father are not for the weak-minded and selfishly controlled. Being a good husband, good father, and good member of society takes work, perseverance, self-control, and selflessness.*

I believe nearly all fathers want to be good fathers to their children, but many lack the skills and training due to poor role models in their own lives. Too many men have lacked Godly role models to pattern their lives and actions after. We see the evidence of these shortcomings everywhere we turn.

The effects of divorce and single parenthood on children and society

When husbands and wives live out their lives in love according to God's design, we see healthy marriages and healthy families. But according to statistics, we see that over half our population of married couples has abandoned God's design to follow their own selfish paths, thereby ending in divorce. Since my first marriage ended in divorce, I must include myself in this group. My wife and I considered our own pain more than what it would do to our children. I sorely regret that. For us, our children were both college age and we thought it would be easier on them at that age. In retrospect, I have come to realize it doesn't matter what age children are – dissolving a marriage causes lasting damage to those divorcing and to all their relationships that is difficult to calculate and more hurtful than we can envision before divorcing. Therefore, I again caution you, if you ever consider divorce to relieve your pain, reconsider and do everything possible to repair your marriage and commit to making it last and improve. I say that not just for your sake, but especially for the sake of your children.

In Chapter 3 dealing with marriage, we discovered that God hates divorce. God revealed through His prophet Malachi that He hates divorce because He desires Godly offspring from our marriages. The dysfunction caused by divorce to children can be pronounced and long-lasting. Therefore, if you are a married man, take the responsibility to do the necessary work to mature your marriage and family relationships to keep them healthy. Your children are counting on you and trusting you for stability and guidance. Take that responsibility seriously by consciously focusing on the needs of your wife and family above your own. God will take care of your needs if you will do your part as He has instructed.

Since today we have large numbers of divorced couples, couples living together outside of wedlock, and large numbers of single parents who never married, we can assume we have many millions of children not receiving proper instruction in God's Word or enjoying the examples of healthy marriage relationships. This being the case, is it any wonder we see so many young people making poor life choices and living worldly lives separated from God.

Added to that drama are all the re-marriages with step-children involved, of which I am one of them. I have found that being a step-father is probably the most challenging role I have had or ever will have in life, other than marriage itself. From conversations with other men, the common experiences seem to be pretty similar. If you try to treat your step-children as your own and discipline them as your own, you will likely encounter instances where your wife steps in and makes it clear that they are "her" children – not yours. This not only affects the relationships you have with your step-children and own children, but heavily influences your relationship with your wife. That is just another reason God hates divorce – it tears something apart that was meant to last a lifetime, and it can cause conflict in your future marriage. If you are a step-father and were able to easily blend into that role, I praise God for that success! More often than not, I believe you will find it a challenge.

If you need counseling to help achieve a fulfilling marriage and successful family, please get the help you need. Life does not have to be lived in anger, disappointment, and bitterness. Christ died to give us an abundant life filled with peace, joy, and contentment. If anything is stealing that gift from you, pray, connect with Godly Christian men for support, read God's Word daily for strength, comfort, and direction and get individual, marriage, and family counseling if you need it; then, let go of your cares and let God work out the details over time

The most important thing you can do is remain loving, patient, and kind no matter what – don't let negative circumstances manipulated by Satan or your old emotional wounds steal the gift of peace Christ died to give you. Christ has already given us peace as believers; it is our job to hang on to it. If you are not a believer, I tell you with all truth and sincerity that Christ is the only way, truth, and life. He is the giver of peace. I remember seeing a bumper sticker that read, "No Jesus – No Peace. Know Jesus – Know Peace." That is most certainly the truth.

The results of fathers neglecting their responsibilities

Because many fathers and husbands have not assumed the responsibility assigned them by God, which is to be the spiritual leader of the household, mothers have, in many cases, had to assume responsibilities they were never intended to carry as we covered in the chapter on marriage. Besides mothers, day care centers, school teachers, Sunday school programs, government programs, and etcetera have tried to fill the responsibility and accountability gap that men and fathers in particular have many times neglected. I see this as a major contributor to the catastrophic breakdown in societies around the world.

It was never God's intention for women, world outreach organizations, and Sunday school programs to replace the father's role. Men are called to be the leaders in their homes and society. Being a leader assumes you are out front showing the way by example – working hard, living Godly, and being a responsible husband, father, and member of society. Families and societies thrive when Godly men lead.

Dealing with failures

I remember a number of specific instances where I wish I had acted differently with my children, especially my oldest. As I have gained experience and more understanding, I realize there were times when I thought I was doing the right thing when in hindsight I see how much better I could have handled situations. Recently, I found myself apologizing to my son for some of those instances where I wish I had handled situations better in his childhood. He was so kind and gracious. He told me he couldn't remember the situations I was feeling sorry for and said I had done so many things right that I shouldn't worry about the few things I might have done less than perfect. I say that to help you understand that you won't do everything right. Our children allow us to make mistakes if they know we love them and are doing our best. As they are growing, you may not feel they love you at times or appreciate you, but if you consistently show them Godly love and support, and apologize to them when you are wrong, they will in all likelihood look back and appreciate that effort and acknowledge it in their adult years, if not sooner.

You are not perfect and will never be perfect – that is why Jesus, the perfect Lamb of God, shed His blood to pay for all your mistakes, every one of them. When you make a mistake, confess it to God and the individual involved; then, claim the forgiveness Jesus' death purchased for you. Once you confess your sin, God the Father again sees you as perfect in His sight through the filter of His Son's Blood. Do not live in guilt or shame over the past or current mistakes – it has already been paid for and forgiven. So when you blow it and realize it, confess your sin to receive forgiveness and then go on to change whatever behaviors have been causing you or your children pain.

Lead by example – showing our children the way

<u>III John 1: 4 (KJV – *emphasis added*)</u>
"I have no greater joy than to hear that my children walk in truth."

As a parent, I want more than anything for my children to walk in the ways of the Lord – in truth. I want them to develop a close personal relationship with Jesus because I know from my own experience that He is the source of our peace, joy, prosperity, contentment, and help. You may be the parent, but your children are just on loan from your Father in Heaven to care for and train up into Godly adults. As parents, we become teachers, and our goal should be to point our children to the truth, which is Jesus the Christ.

Truth
The quality or state of being faithful
Sincerity in character, action, and faith
Something that is fact

Jesus said in John 14:6, *"I am the way, the truth, and the life. No one comes to the Father except through Me"* (NKJV – *emphasis added*)

Jesus is truth.   Jesus is faithful.   Jesus is sincere.   Jesus is fact.

Since we automatically become teachers when our children are born, it is important to understand what a teacher (father) is and what we are responsible for teaching.

Teach
To show – guide – direct – instruct
To cause to know something
To accustom to some action or attitudes
To direct, instruct, or train by precept, example, or experience

Lead
To guide or conduct someone along a way – show the way to a place especially by going with or in advance
To go with usually at the head and direct the operations of
To bring by reasoning, cogency, or other influence to some conclusion or condition

Cogency
Having the power of compelling or constraining
Appealing forcibly to the mind or reason

Precept
A command or principle intended as a general rule of action
A written order or mandate issued by legally constituted authority to a person commanding or authorizing him to do something

As fathers (teachers), we have the cogency to either lead and guide our children into a relationship with our Lord and Savior, Jesus Christ, or down a destructive, ungodly, worldly path. The Lord's precepts are readily available in the Bible for us to teach, and Jesus commands us to teach His ways to our children so they can grow up to enjoy the abundant life He offers. So when you teach, you should teach with authority the precepts (commands and principles) of God.

<u>Proverbs 22: 6 (NIV – *emphasis added*)</u>
"Train a child in the way he should go, and when he is old he will not turn from it."

What is the way a child should go? Again, I want to remind you that Jesus said in John 14:6, *"I am the way, the truth, and the life. No one comes to the Father except through Me"*

<u>Way</u>
A thoroughfare used or designed for traveling or transportation from place to place
A course of action
A method of attaining or accomplishing something

Jesus is the way. Jesus took the action necessary to become the thoroughfare through which we can attain eternal life and an abundant life on earth.

<u>Life</u>
The quality that distinguishes a vital and functional being from a dead body or purely chemical matter
A spiritual form of eternal existence transcending physical death
Something held to be essential to animate existence or livelihood
One that inspires or excites spirit and vigor and is usually held to provide a principal basis for enjoyment or success

Now, as far as the way our children should go when it relates to their calling in life. Biblically, our duty as a father is to help bring out their natural bent installed in them by God. Many times, fathers especially attempt to mold and direct their children in the way they think they should go. Or they sometimes push their children to achieve dreams they failed to achieve. Don't make that mistake. Instead, help them discover their God-given gifts and calling so they can live a fulfilled and content life doing what God has put in them to do.

Godly versus worldly

God calls us to separate ourselves from the world and live spiritually in Christ. The apostle Paul said those who belong to Christ have crucified their natural worldly lusts and desires and have become new creations. So what does it mean to be Godly versus worldly? Again we turn to Webster's dictionary.

<u>Godly / Godliness</u>
Of, relating to, or emanating from God
Reverencing God: obedient to the will of God from love and reverence for His character

Conforming one's life to the revealed character and purpose of God: righteousness

Worldly / worldly-minded
Earthly rather than heavenly or spiritual
Interested in or concerned with the enjoyments of this present existence
Devoted to the world and its pursuits
Devoted to or engrossed in worldly interests
Having one's thoughts or interests set upon things of this world

To experience the most abundant life possible, focus your mind on heavenly and spiritual things and conform yourself to God's revealed character of righteousness. Encourage your children to do the same.

We teach more by our example than we do by our words. Do your children see you going to church, being involved in your church and community, helping others in need, and living a Godly lifestyle? Or do they see you frequent bars and casinos, tell dirty jokes, frequently angry and degrading others, and the like? God calls us to live holy, and that is especially true for fathers and church leaders. Holy does not mean we will achieve perfection. Holy means we live life dedicated to loving God, our wife, our children, and others that we influence. The fact is we can only find lasting joy, peace, prosperity, and contentment when keeping our focus on God and seeking to live a holy life.

If you are a Christian man, whether you realize it or not, the unsaved world and your children watch you and judge the character of God based on your actions. Christians give the world stability. When someone has a need or faces a crisis, they know where to go. They seek out those who have an obvious relationship with Jesus Christ because they see the power in that relationship, even if they do not fully understand it. The world sees the power of Christ and the power God wield through Christians, even if they refuse to acknowledge it. That is why it is so important for us to walk in the Spirit and "walk the talk," as the saying goes. If you take an inventory of all the outreach organizations in the world, you will find most are Christian-based.

Called to teach

Normally when considering the call to teach, we are referring to formal teaching professions in the academic school system or Sunday school system. However, as parents; especially fathers, we are automatically called by God to teach our children.

Call
A divine vocation or prompting to a special service or duty
A strong inner prompting to undertake a particular course of action or to enter a particular type of vocation

To become driven
To hold responsible

Vocation
A summons from God to an individual or group to undertake the obligations and per-
form the duties of a particular task or function in life
A divine call to a place or service to others in accordance with the divine plan
A task or function to which one is called by God

We men are called to lead our children into Godliness. Our children seeing the
fruit of the Spirit produced through us will likely be the predominant way we will lead
them into their own personal relationship with Christ. And as our children grow in
their relationship to God and man, we will see the peace and grace of God sustaining
their lives and relationships.

To know how well you are walking with God, look again to 1 Corinthians chapter
13, and Galatians 5:22-23. As you mature in your walk with God and allow the Holy
Spirit to guide you, you should see the behaviors listed in Galatians become more
evident in your life – *love (charity), joy, peace, patience (long-suffering), kindness,
goodness, faithfulness, gentleness, and self-control.*

The seriousness of teaching your children

Matthew 18: 2-6, 10 (NIV – *emphasis added*)
*"He (Jesus) called a little child and had him stand among them. And He said:
'I tell you the truth, unless you change and become like little children, you will never
enter the kingdom of heaven. Therefore, whoever humbles himself like this child is the
greatest in the kingdom of heaven. And whoever welcomes a little child like this in my
name welcomes me. But if anyone causes one of these little ones who believe in me
to sin, it would be better for him to have a large millstone hung around his neck and
to be drowned in the depths of the sea. See that you do not look down on one of these
little ones; for I tell you that their angels in heaven always see the face of my Father
in heaven."*

Children rely on adults to lead them. Ironically, Jesus called His disciples little children, too, so we are not only talking about small children in age but also in spiritual
growth. As men and fathers, we have a responsibility to "learn and live" the gospel message so our children can learn from our example.

Youth are looking for God but finding many gods instead

People worship many things – wealth, power, celebrities, sex, sports heroes, drugs, cars; the list is endless. Whoever or whatever you put your trust in becomes your god. If you trust in drugs or alcohol to escape your pain and troubles, then they have become your gods. If you emotionally connect yourself to a celebrity by emulating them to boost your self-esteem, then they have become your god. If you are feeling high when your favorite sports team wins and down when they lose, then they have become a god that you look to for building your self-esteem.

The things we worship can come in very subtle forms, and many times we don't recognize it as idol worship because society accepts and promotes an endless variety of idol worship, usually for financial gain at our expense. As we look at the definitions for God and god, you may think of more gods our society worships.

God
The holy, infinite, and eternal spiritual reality presented in the Bible as the creator, sustainer, judge, righteous sovereign, and redeemer of the universe who acts with power in history in carrying out His purpose
The unchangeably perfect Being that is the first and final cause of the universe
Reality as opposed to appearance

god
A being of more than human attributes and powers
An artificial or natural object (as a carved idol or an animal or tree) that is thought to be the seat of divine powers, the expression of a divine personality, or itself a supernatural or divine agency
A person or thing that is honored as a god or deified; something held to be of supreme value
One who wields great or despotic power
A human being of extraordinary attractive physical stature

I'm sure after reading the definitions for small god you can think of many worldly gods that people follow after or worship. Everyone worships and serves someone or something. That someone or something is either God or other gods. I am including definitions from Webster's Dictionary for worship also. I believe after getting a fuller understanding of what worship is, you will see how easily we can be influenced to spend time worshipping false gods daily.

Worship
A set of ceremonies, prayers, or other religious forms by which reverent love and allegiance to God is expressed.

Ardent, humble devotion
To love or pursue devotedly

Ardent
Expressing or characterized by warmth of passion, emotion, or desire
Displaying or characterized by strong enthusiasm or devotion

What things in the world do you see people strongly pursuing or strongly devoted to? What are you strongly pursuing or devoted to? What are you encouraging your children to strongly pursue or be devoted to? We obviously have responsibilities in this world that we are accountable for fulfilling, and God has given us many things in this life to enjoy. The problem comes with our focus. Are you focused on God and serving others while you enjoy the many blessings He brings into your life? If so, you will have peace and be content. If you are focused on worldly pleasures and getting for yourself, you will find yourself often anxious, disappointed, and discontent. That is a good test. Ask yourself if you feel peace and feel at rest. If you are diligently seeking a closer relationship with God, you should.

It should be obvious from the definitions that every human being worships someone or something. You either devotedly pursue God or gods. Blessings come with a devoted pursuit of God. Curses come with a devoted pursuit of gods. Our children need to know this truth; and our primary responsibility is to point them to Jesus.

Making God's Word real for children

2 Timothy 3: 16 (NKJV – *emphasis added*)
"All scripture is given by inspiration of God, and is profitable for doctrine, for reproof, for correction, for instruction in righteousness: that the man of God may be perfect, thoroughly furnished unto all good works."

It is important to make God's Word relevant to every situation in your children's lives so they learn they can turn to God for all of their needs. I would suggest that most adults and children put their faith in their own talents and abilities or in another person or worldly system rather than in God. As we are praying to God for help with our lips, our heart is many times anxious and our mind is trying to come up with a solution to our problem because many times we don't trust God to actually handle the problem we are praying about. We give God lip service while we depend on ourselves to come up with the solution.

Putting our trust in ourselves, our government, our friends, our family, or any other human being or system will always lead to eventual disappointment because only God in Christ Jesus is fully dependable and faithful to protect, care for, and love us consistently. He is never too busy or preoccupied to meet our need twenty-four hours a day.

When that truth takes root in our heart, we are then able to truly trust God with our problems and rest in His peace as we patiently wait for Him to act.

God's living word, the Bible, provides us with all the Godly information we need for encouragement, instruction, comfort, and guidance. It is God's own Testimony concerning His nature, His general will for us, His redemptive sacrifice, and plans for the future. God's Word truly is "living," and as we seek a closer relationship with the Lord, He continually increases our wisdom, understanding, and knowledge through His written Testimony. That is why it is so important for fathers and teachers of the Word to spend time in it daily. If you want to be a REAL man, a huge step in that process is becoming intimately connected to Jesus – the *"author and finisher of our faith."*

Ways to be an effective father-teacher of God's Word?

To help you along your REAL manhood journey, I am including thoughts based on my experience. I am confident they will help you in your own maturing process.

- Walk the talk – do as you say.
- Pray as you study your Bible that God would open your understanding and reveal what He wants to get across to you and your children.
- Pray that the Lord would open the hearts, minds, and souls of your children to receive His daily instruction.
- Pray with your children daily while they are still at home and under your care.
- Talk to your children like people – don't talk "at" them. Respect your children and they are more likely to respect you.
- Your children need love and compassion – let your children see that you care about them. If you do anything that you would apologize to an adult for, then apologize to your child. Be as polite to your children as you would be to others.
- Teach from your heart – your children need to see how important Jesus is to you.
- Use examples from your own life whenever possible to show how the Lord has been with you, helped you, talked to you, guided you, and never forsaken you.
- Don't be afraid to cry or show emotion. Jesus was more man than any of us will ever come close to being and He wept on a number of occasions out of love and compassion.
- Use plenty of Scripture in your teaching to show God's Word has practical and relevant answers to everyday problems and questions.
- Be consistent in your discipline and don't threaten anything you won't enforce.
- Work as a team with your wife. Don't let the children see or hear the two of you disagree concerning their discipline or correction. Children quickly pick up on this and can use it to manipulate you.

-Remember, your main goal in teaching God's Word is to lead your children into a closer relationship with Jesus Christ. Teaching church traditions, Bibles stories, facts from the Bible, and memorization should all be geared toward the ultimate goal of bringing your children into a closer relationship with Christ Jesus. That is why you need to make God's Word relevant to their lives. Just telling them not to do something because they shouldn't isn't a good enough answer, in my opinion – they need to know why they shouldn't do certain things and why they should do others.

-Conform your life to the revealed character of God (as revealed in the fruit of the Spirit) to be an effective leader in your family.

-Jesus sent the Holy Spirit to bring to remembrance all that He taught. What He taught is in the Bible. If you don't know God's Word, you won't know if your thoughts are your own, from Satan, or from God.

Our source of wisdom and understanding

Proverbs 9: 10 (NIV – *emphasis added*)
"The fear of the Lord is the beginning of wisdom, and knowledge of the Holy One is understanding."

Proverbs 2: 1-11 (NIV – *emphasis added*)
"My son, if you accept my words and store up my commands within you, turning your ear to wisdom and applying your heart to understanding, and if you call out for insight and cry aloud for understanding, and if you look for it as for silver and search for it as for hidden treasure, then you will understand the fear of the Lord, and find the knowledge of God. For the Lord gives wisdom, and from His mouth come knowledge and understanding. He holds victory in store for the upright; He is a shield to those whose walk is blameless, for He guards the course of the just and protects the way of His faithful ones. Then you will understand what is right and just and fair...wisdom will enter your heart, and knowledge will be pleasant to your soul. Discretion will protect you and understanding will guard you."

To be a successful father and leader, you need wisdom and understanding. That wisdom and understanding originates in God. God's wisdom and understanding will lead you and guide you into being a good father to your children and a good role model for other youth.

What should a child expect from a father?
What should a father expect from a child?

I believe as you read the partial list of answers I provide, you will begin to see how important your role as a man and a father is.

<u>What should a child expect from his or her father?</u>
To instruct them in the ways of God as revealed in the Bible
To give words of encouragement
To discipline (not punish) when needed to keep them on the right track
To supply their basic needs (food, shelter, clothing)
To be honest and live with high integrity
To protect them from harm
To be truthful and dependable
To give gifts that make their lives more fulfilled and enjoyable
To be kind, gentle, and self-controlled
To look out for their best interests
To challenge them to mature in responsibility and accountability
To be understanding, patient, kind, and gentle
To reward them for obedience and hard work
To forgive their mistakes and unconditionally love them
To be available to them when they need help or have questions

<u>What should a father expect from his children?</u>
Obedience
Respect

To be a REAL man and father takes work. If you are a REAL man according to God's definition, good for you – keep up the good work and keep seeking God for continued growth because you will never reach God's example of perfection. But your goal should be to daily continue traveling in that direction through the power of the Holy Spirit. Determine in your heart to mentor other men, helping them improve in their fathering skills and grow their relationships with God.

If you are one of those men who has been lax in his responsibilities, or abandoned them all together, it is not too late for you to remedy your poor choices. You can never re-create the past to make your mistakes turn out differently, but you can decide from this moment forward to dedicate your life to the Lord Jesus Christ and begin the process of becoming the man and father God has called you to be. You can repent (turn around, change your ways), receive God's forgiveness, and start seeing changes from this moment forward. So if this is you, surrender to Jesus, admit you have messed up, ask Him to come into your heart and change you. Once you have done that, you will begin seeing changes in your life as you continue to listen to His voice and let the Holy Spirit guide you. Connect to a good church where you can grow spiritually and contribute your God-given talents and abilities to help the rest of the body of Christ.

The empty nest

As my children were growing, I was very active in their lives. I didn't realize how much so until they were grown and started leaving home for college. The empty nest syndrome, as it is called, caught me by surprise and affected me more than I expected.

I soon discovered that I suddenly had much more time on my hands and had to recreate my life to fill in the time that had been consumed by my children. For some of you, this might seem like a welcome relief to look forward to. For me, it was filled with mixed emotions. I felt proud seeing my children grow, become more independent, and go off to form their own lives, but I sincerely missed spending time with them and enjoying all the extracurricular activities they were involved with at school and church and other outside interest. I address this simply to prepare you for that day and also to remind you to keep your relationship with your wife alive and well. It is not uncommon for marriages to end in divorce after twenty-five to thirty years when the kids leave home, so I encourage you again to maintain a healthy marriage through any means necessary so you can enjoy your years with your wife after kids.

Concluding comments

I have found fatherhood to be a tremendous joy, but also at times a seemingly overwhelming responsibility as my children grew into adulthood. At times, I felt like the weight of the world was on my shoulders. That is when I turned heavily into God's Word, the Bible, for comfort, guidance, and strength. That is the point in a marriage when I think too many men make poor choices to avoid the adversities of life. Rather than seek God for the strength, wisdom, and understanding to mature as husbands and fathers, too many men head for bars, drugs, hobbies, or other avenues of escape in an attempt to temporarily kill and forget their struggles and challenges. But these worldly routes never bring permanent relief. After a day or night of temporary worldly relief, they wake up the next morning with the same struggles. Alcohol, drugs, hobbies, or whatever other god you turn to in your times of stress will not provide lasting relief – only Jesus can do that. In His Testimony, God says He longs to be compassionate to us; He just patiently waits for us to seek him for mercy, grace, and comfort.

Also realize your struggles predominantly come from pride – wanting things your way. In a marriage and family, you cannot often have your own way. There are many needs to consider, and as a man, you are responsible for most of them – just as Christ is responsible for the needs of His bride and family (the church of believers).

It was not easy raising children to adulthood, but as I sought God for strength and direction, He provided me with the strength, insights, and wisdom I needed to continually mature as a father and face each day. I know from my own experience that letting God take the reins to your heart and mind is the best route to becoming the father and leader you want to be deep inside. There are few things as rewarding as hearing your children tell you that you have been a good father. I know I have made mistakes, but I thank God that He continually forgives, and I thank my children for their love and forgiveness, knowing that I have always acted with best intentions.

I have heard people say through pride that good intentions don't get the job done, but our intentions are exactly what God looks at. Our intentions (motives) come from our heart, and our heart's intent is what God cares about. Sometimes, we make mistakes while proceeding with right motives. When we increase in wisdom and understanding, however, and recognize our errors, we should quit repeating them. Part of maturing is not repeating poor choices. Too often we hear men making excuses for their poor choices and behaviors instead of admitting they sinned and repenting (changing their behavior). You can never mature in character or grow closer to God until you confess your sin. With that confession, you receive forgiveness, mercy, and grace.

Children need Godly examples, men. Therefore, I reemphasize that you cannot become the REAL man you want to be inside without maturing your relationship with our Lord and Savior, Jesus the Christ. True wisdom and understanding come only from God above. We need Godly men to properly instruct children in the ways of God because they are the ones who will rise up to lead in the future. They need you to be all that God created you to be! They need REAL men in their lives.

Chapter 6

The costs and benefits of REAL manhood

esus warns us to count the cost of following Him before making that decision. If we turn back after making that commitment, the Bible says God will take no pleasure in us. In fact, we are told we will be worse off afterward than before if we turn our back on Him after accepting Him as our Lord and Savior.

From Luke 14: 26-35 (*TLB – emphasis added*)
"Anyone who wants to be my follower must love Me far more than he does his own father, mother, wife, children, brother, or sister – yes, more than his own life – otherwise he cannot be My disciple. And no one can be My disciple who does not carry his own cross and follow Me. But do not begin until you count the cost. For who would begin construction of a building without first getting estimates and then checking to see if he has enough money to pay the bills? Otherwise he might complete only the foundation before running out of funds. And then how everyone would laugh! Or what king would ever dream of going to war without first sitting down with his counselors and discussing whether his army of 10,000 is strong enough to defeat the 20,000 men who are marching against him? If the decision is negative, then while the enemy troops are still far away, he will send a truce team to discuss terms of peace. So no one can become My disciple unless he first sits down and counts his blessings and then renounces them all for Me. What good is salt that has lost its saltiness? Flavorless salt is fit for nothing – not even for fertilizer. It is worthless and must be thrown out. Listen well, if you would understand my meaning?"

Since making a decision to follow Christ is a serious matter, I want you to understand the costs of following Him so you can make an informed decision.

Relinquishing pride

A major cost in following Christ is pride. What makes this difficult is that most men are full of it. I have elaborated on pride in previous chapters and its devastating effects on relationships and its caustic effects on the world at large. But because pride is such a hindrance to our relationship with God and others, I want to briefly reiterate the importance of humbling ourselves before God and man.

Psalm 51: 17 (KJV – *emphasis added*)
"The sacrifices of God are a broken spirit; a broken and a contrite heart, O God, thou wilt not despise."

Why would God, our Father and Creator, want to see our hearts and spirits broken? To more fully understand what God means by broken spirit and contrite heart, we turn once again to Webster's Dictionary.

Broken
Tamed and trained
Subdued; humbled
Shattered
Broken-hearted: grievously sad
Crushed by grief
Not functioning

Contrite
Repentant for one's sins or inadequacies
Sincere remorse for wrong-doing

With our spirit broken, we tend to reach a teachable moment, realizing we are not in control of our circumstances. We cannot control other peoples' behavior to maintain our constant comfort level. We cannot always prevent the death of our loved ones or close friends. We seldom can control very little other than our reaction to circumstances. Events in our lives that cause our hearts to break are many times our best opportunities to reach out to God and feel His peace, comfort, and strength. As He repeatedly brings us successfully through our adversities, we come to realize over time that God is dependable and faithful. In fact, we find that Jesus is the only one who is always dependable and faithful. Trusting in ourselves or other people always leads to eventual disappointment because none of us can deliver every time.

Many times, until we have traumatic or heart-breaking moments in our lives, we tend to run around pridefully looking out for our own selfish interests. God, through His goodness, sometimes allows these tragic events in our lives to give us the opportunity to reach out to Him and receive comfort and strength through His mercy and grace.

Since the world promotes pride and rebellion against God, until you develop a close intimate relationship with Jesus (Father, Son, and Holy Ghost), you will probably not recognize your pride because you will be doing, acting, and thinking like the world around you. Seeking God through reading the Bible, prayer, good Biblical teaching, attending church regularly (at least weekly), and fellowshipping with mature Christians will help you recognize pride in all its subtleness and wean yourself from it.

Wise King Solomon concluded at the end of the book of Ecclesiastes that our entire duty in life is to fear God and obey His commandments. The kind of fear he is referring to is having an awesome respect for God. Until our spirits are broken, I do not believe we can truly have an awesome respect for God, or respect our fellow human beings.

When I think back to my military experience in the United States Army, and going through basic training, I recognize that part of the training was a sustained effort to break our wills so we would learn to obey orders without questioning. Our instructors taught us skills to help us defeat our enemy, provided mental and physical conditioning to prepare us for battle, and taught us teamwork. Our military forces would be pretty useless if everyone decided they were going to do things their own way – not listening to the orders of their commanding officers and our country's leaders. In order for any organization to succeed, its members must be united in purpose and all the members must be willing to obey their leaders.

The family of God is similar to branches of the Armed Forces. We are in a spiritual battle and the only power we have to fight that battle is through the power of God's Holy Spirit. The first step in winning our battles is accessing that power by letting go of our pride – humbling ourselves before God. As we humble ourselves before God, He guides us through His Spirit, giving us wisdom and understanding to make good and right decisions. As we continue walking in the light of the truth taught through His Spirit, we feel our peace and contentment continually increase. Through that humbling process, we become increasingly more like God and He rewards that obedience with spiritual and material blessings.

To condition ourselves for our walk with the Lord, we must read God's Word, remain physically pure and fit, and fellowship with mature members of the body of Christ. Once prepared for battle, we will be ready to resist our enemy, Satan and his angels, and enjoy the abundant life Christ died to give us.

Self-realization

Another cost of following Christ is learning how flawed we are. The Holy Spirit will open up your understanding, reveal your true self, and start perfecting you, making you more Christ-like. That can be a painful process – painful in the respect that you see how flawed you are as you come to feel deep remorse for your prideful behavior.

I think it important to point out here how God works in His perfecting process to help you distinguish the voice of God from the voice of Satan. When God is perfecting you and revealing your flaws, He does it tenderly and gently. You may find yourself weeping and feeling remorse as your Father in Heaven gently reveals areas of your life that need correcting. God NEVER perfects you by making you feel guilty. Satan is the accuser and slanderer – he slanders you, God, and everyone else in your life. When you hear a voice in your head condemning you, slandering you, or slandering others you love in an effort to anger and separate you from God and each other, that voice is Satan's – God will never do that.

God's correction is tender and makes you weep with remorse – not guilt. Jesus died to reconcile us to the Father and remove our guilt and shame, so if you are seeking the Lord and seeking to walk His path, you will not hear Him condemning you. When those condemning and slanderous thoughts come, take them captive and dismiss them in the name of Jesus through the Blood of the Lamb (Christ Jesus). Then replace those slanderous thoughts with truthful thoughts and promises from God's Holy Word.

Most of us like to think others cause our pain, but our pain comes from inside in the way we respond to things done to us that we don't like or don't think are fair. We like to have things our way. When they don't go our way, we tend to blame other people for hurting us. In reality, we usually need to learn how to respond to things differently. Our true enemy is within – we tend to be our own worst enemies.

The Bible reveals that we will experience trials and temptations throughout our life. How we respond to them reveals the level of our maturity. Mature people respond with the fruit of the Holy Spirit as revealed in Galatians 5:22-23 – with *love (charity), joy, peace, longsuffering (patience), kindness, goodness, faithfulness, gentleness, and self-control.* Use that list of Godly fruit as your litmus test to see how you are doing in your spiritual development.

Lifestyle and friends

Other costs of becoming a REAL man may be your lifestyle and friends. Once you have accepted the Lord Jesus as your Savior and been liberated from illusion and ignorance by the Holy Spirit, it may become necessary to quit associating with friends whose lifestyles are not conformed to the will of God. The Holy Spirit will reveal to you those relationships which must be severed for you to continue on your spiritual growth and perfecting path. Even though unhealthy relationships may not condemn you in and of themselves, they tend to lead you away from God. If you fail to sever those relationships, you will forfeit numerous blessings. God may love you, but He only rewards you when you diligently seek a closer relationship with Him and put your trust in Him.

If you claim Christ as your Savior but it produces no change in your life, or spiritual growth, then it shows you have not made a commitment to Christ. Without that commitment, you will not experience the abundant life that He died to give you. Jesus said on a number of occasions **if** we love Him, we will obey Him – obedience is proof of our love. He also said **if** we love and obey Him, the Father would give us anything we asked for in line with His will. Therefore, if you are not obedient to Christ's commands, it shows that you do not love Him, and He cannot bless you because of the restrictions He has placed on Himself. God will not reward bad behavior. So if you want to experience the abundant life God has reserved for you, you must commit your life to Him and surrender your agenda to Him – allowing Him to take the lead in teaching you and guiding you through His Holy Spirit.

Sacrificing good things for the sake of others

You may have to give up things that are perfectly okay in God's eyes for you to do. Yes, there are things you may be doing now that are perfectly okay, as the apostle Paul pointed out, but you may have to give them up to prevent one weaker in the faith from stumbling in his or her faith. Why, you ask? Sometimes, we may need to give up things because they may cause another Christian to stumble or sin due to their tender conscience or weaker faith.

One example I use cautiously is drinking alcohol. I say cautiously because I know this to be a decisive issue in the body of Christ, and I myself believe that alcohol should be avoided because of all the damage it obviously causes in peoples' lives. But it does serve as a good example that everyone can probably relate to. Some in the body of Christ believe drinking alcohol is a sin and should be avoided, while others in the church believe there is nothing wrong with drinking alcohol as long as it is done in moderation. If you are of the mindset drinking alcohol is okay, it can become a problem if you drink alcohol in the presence of your Christian friend who believes drinking alcohol is a sin, and through the passage of time, you entice him to drink alcohol. Believing in his heart that he just committed sin, he spends his time in anguish feeling guilty and rejected by God. Now, even though your conscience is clear, he just committed sin and you led him or her into it.

That is just one example. The point here is that we should be led by the Holy Spirit to be sensitive to the needs of others and what will benefit their soul and walk with God. Without compromising our own belief system, we must keep in mind that our top priority is always to love God with our whole heart, mind, soul, and strength and to love our neighbor as our self. That means we put our desires second in relation to the needs of others.

Sometimes, life just does not seem fair, but when we accept and acknowledge Christ as our God and Savior, we should no longer live to please ourselves – we should be living to please Christ who died to provide for us a more abundant life now and forevermore. It wasn't fair for a sinless Christ to pay our debt with His life either. But He did. One thing I can tell you – you will not miss habits or things you willingly give up to benefit others or to please God. The key is to give them up willingly. If you give them up grudgingly, you may come to resent those you sacrifice for, and you may resent God for your grudging choice. Whatever you do, do it willingly out of your love for Christ and others, not out of guilt or to feel more holy and acceptable to God. God knows and judges the motives of your heart. God is looking for willing and pure hearts. He is not impressed by you attempting to earn His acceptance and favor by simply following a set of rules you grudgingly submit to.

Practice living your life to meet the needs of others without concern for your own wants, and you will find God is able and willing to fulfill the good desires of your heart so you will never be lacking anything good. As you practice self-sacrifice for the right reasons – because you sincerely care about others and love God – rather than to earn God's approval, or the approval of others, you will find yourself satisfied and living in the peace and contentment that the world at large cannot attain or fully comprehend.

Personal sacrifices

Now, let's do a little exercise. I would like you to list behaviors you have given up, or would like to give up – behaviors that rob you of peace, joy, love, and contentment. These are things you know are holding you back from growing closer to God and others in your life.

_____

_____

_____

_____

_____

_____

_____

Now, if you give up something, you must replace it with something or those old habits and behaviors will return. Jesus once told a parable concerning this phenomenon. So now list new habits and behaviors you want to replace the old with to help you walk in love to God and neighbor.

_____

_____

_____

_____

_____

_____

_____

Summarizing the cost to becoming a REAL man

So what is your cost for following Christ? Your cost is to give up all the things in your life that cause harm to yourself or to others. Your cost is to give up your pride and selfishness, letting the Holy Spirit lead, guide, and take care of you. Your cost is to love God, love yourself, and love others as much as you love yourself. Your cost is to accept all the good things God has to offer you. Your cost is to look at yourself as you really are and to esteem others above yourself. Your cost is to be Christ-like. Does that sound like too much to ask?

As your Great Shepherd, Jesus invites you to cast all your cares on Him. Jesus is capable of carrying your overwhelming burdens for you, no matter what they are. So count the cost and realize the benefits you will receive infinitely outweigh the costs.

The benefits of becoming a REAL man God's way

REAL manhood is found in Christ alone. Since following Christ is not always easy, and it doesn't keep us from experiencing trials, pains, or temptations, then why follow Him? If we choose to follow Christ and submit to His authority over every area of our life, then there must be some benefits that we receive from that. If there are no benefits, why do it?

Freedom from illusions and ignorance

One huge benefit is Jesus' promise that the Holy Spirit will lead us into all truth and that truth will set us free from ignorance and illusion – freedom that is part of salvation. Before Christ's crucifixion, He told His disciples He would send the Holy Spirit to comfort them, remind them of everything He had said, and lead them into right living.

Without the Holy Spirit giving us direction, we will unwittingly follow the path the world lays out before us through advertising and media propaganda. Or, even more likely, we will follow our own perverted selfish inclinations and do things only to please ourselves or those closest to us – not caring about how our lifestyle affects others. But if we relinquish control of our spirit to the Holy Spirit of God, we can depend on Him to take us where we should go and show us what we should do.

That does not mean life will always be easy, however. We still have our flesh to contend with. Our own selfish desires will compete with our re-born spirit for control. We can also expect Satan to be persistently attempting to deceive us out of our faith. So, as with the apostle Paul, we will face a constant battle against spiritual forces we cannot see. However, many times we end up being our own worst enemy without Satan having to lift a finger because our sinful nature simply wants its own way. It is when we fully commit to Christ that Satan becomes our worst enemy; until then, it is many times our own sinful nature that leads us astray.

Satan cannot make us do anything, and God won't. When Christ fulfilled His mission by dying on the cross, He broke Satan's power over us. As believers, we now have the power of the God's Spirit and His truth available within us. We don't have to rely on our own understanding. We are no match for Satan and his illusions when we rely on our own understanding or worldly wisdom for guidance; we must rely on the Holy Spirit's guidance.

God becomes our friend

Another benefit of following Christ is the fact that He (Christ) becomes our friend. Jesus told His disciples during His last night on earth before going to the cross that He no longer called them servants, but friends. They were now friends because He had revealed His and the Father's identity to them, and they had believed and obeyed Him. Remember when Satan comes to you with slanderous thoughts about yourself or anyone else, you, as a committed believer, are a friend of God. With God on your side, you have the power within you to resist these devilish mental attacks. With God on your side, you can do all things through Christ who strengthens you, as the apostle Paul pointed out.

When trials and temptations come, as they will, the Word of God, the Holy Bible, tells us that those who wait patiently for God to act are blessed. Therefore, we should be constantly seeking Him and dying to our own selfish nature every day, surrendering our fears and selfish desires. Just as we find comfort and strength through earthly friendships, we should all the more find comfort and strength through our friendship with God – the One who can truly comfort and strengthen us through the days we live. God is an awesome God and able to take care of us, but we need to trust Him to do that.

Special blessings

As a perfect parent who knows us better than we know ourselves, God is also pleased to give us good things that satisfy the desires of our hearts – good and wholesome desires that He puts in our hearts as believers. God is truly the only One who knows how to satisfy us. He created us, gave us each unique talents, abilities, and desires, and when we seek His kingdom and righteousness above everything else, He gives us everything we need and fulfills the desires He has placed within us in His good and perfect timing. All He asks in return is that we be thankful, put our total trust in Him, and patiently wait for Him to act on our behalf as our Good Shepherd.

As you commit your life to God and allow the Holy Spirit to lead, you will find many of your old selfish and self-centered desires change over time, and you will experience peace and contentment as you become more outward focused and less inward focused. God is an outward focused God and has created us to be the same. Peace and contentment come when we become more concerned about meeting the needs of others than we are about satisfying our own endless list of selfish desires.

If fear and anxiety become a regular part of our life, it is only because we have taken our spiritual eyes off the true source of every blessing – Jesus the Christ and God the Father. He is the One who is actually providing our talents and abilities to do our job on a daily basis. He is the One who gives us favor in the eyes of our peers and superiors as we confidently work as if working for Him, which we actually are. It is when we keep our focus on God and His promises that we find favor with God and man. Everything we have. Everything we are. Everything we will ever have or be – gifts from a gracious and loving God. The only way for us to lose our blessings is by fearing man and Satan instead of God.

Two fears

Here I want to talk about the two kinds of fears. The most common definition of fear we embrace is that of being afraid of some impending disaster, pain, or loss. The other type of fear is an awesome respect for someone or something.

Fearing man or Satan generally means that we worry about how they can affect our happiness to make our life less fulfilling. It can also mean, however, that we have an awesome respect for man instead of God, which will keep us separated from God and in a state of discontent and anxiety because man will always let us down at some point. And I believe we all know deep inside we cannot completely depend on any man – even our best friend. That, I believe, is why we spend so much time being fearful if we are not putting our trust in God. We know we are not one hundred percent dependable, and neither is anyone else – only God is fully faithful and dependable.

Fear of God means we have an awesome respect for God – we believe and trust in Him completely, confidently living in peace through thankful and grateful hearts for His constant protection and provision. God does not want His children to be afraid of Him. On the contrary, Jesus said He is gentle and humble and invites us to come to Him with our burdens and cares. God wants us to live in the peace that Christ's death on the cross purchased for us – knowing that God is faithful and true and will never leave us or forsake us. God always comes through, in His perfect timing.

Financial and material benefits

I would now like you to list benefits and blessings you have experienced since surrendering your heart and life to Christ; if you have. If you have been a believing Christian for any length of time, you will find your list is endless. If you are a new believer, or in fact just committing your life to Christ after reading this book, you may not have as large a list yet. But as you reflect on God's goodness in your life, even though you may have been walking in the world's ways, the Holy Spirit will reveal to you how God has always been there providing protection and provision through a multitude of sources and people your entire life.

The Bible says God sends rain (blessings) on the just and unjust. And as I said earlier, the Bible reveals that the goodness of God leads to repentance. That is the defining moment in an unbelievers' life – when he or she realizes that God has been calling and reaching out to them. That is the moment when His tender mercy and grace can cause us to weep uncontrollably because, for the first time, we realize how good He has been to us and how we have rebelled against that goodness.

As you create a list of blessings, include physical, emotional, spiritual, and financial benefits. Many Christians have been deceived into thinking they should not be concerned with money or material possessions and that somehow thinking of such things is ungodly behavior. Not so. God's Word clearly reveals a loving Father who loves doing things for us and giving us material wealth to enjoy when our attitude toward them is right. God wants generous, thankful, and grateful hearts in His children. He gladly blesses those who have pure hearts and motives so they can in turn share that wealth with others to enhance their lives and to spread the Good News of salvation and God's goodness. A poor Christian can barely help himself, let alone anyone else. This idea that Christians should be poor or at least not concerned with money or material possessions is a deception that the devil has only been too happy to propagate among the body of Christ.

God will give you ideas and bring people into your life to accelerate your success and increase your wealth as you follow Him and seek to live a Godly life of love. Either that or he will lead you to a company and job that He has prepared for you to provide for your needs and wants – where you can serve others to the glory of God. Everything you do should be to the glory of God.

Now, here is a chance to start listing the benefits, blessings, and rewards you recognize as coming from God either directly or through other people that God has brought into your life.

_____
_____
_____
_____
_____
_____
_____
_____
_____
_____
_____
_____
_____
_____
_____
_____
_____

Hebrews 11:6 (NKJV – *emphasis added*)
"But without faith it is impossible to please Him, for he who comes to God must believe that He is and that He is a rewarder of those who diligently seek Him"

Many within the Christian church miss out on many of God's blessings because they have never been taught they are available to them. Sadly, I know many Christians who think they are just suppose to buck up and let the devil and life beat them silly all their lives and then they get to go to heaven and live happily ever after with Jesus. Well, my Bible says that Jesus the Christ died to reconcile us to God, give us peace and an overflowing abundant life – now and forever. My Bible says we receive overflowing blessings to enjoy and generously share with others as we diligently seek God and His kingdom.

I know from experience that when we place God first in our life, tithe, and generously give to the spreading of the gospel and doing good to others that God the Father will supply our every need and give us the desires of our heart. God wants us to enjoy an abundant, satisfied life. Contrary to what many Christians and the world seem to believe, God is not against His children being rich or having wealth. God is against pride, greed, envy, selfishness, and covetousness. This perversion of the gospel message continues to rob Christians of blessings to enjoy and share with others.

Most of humanity spends much time thinking about money because it's needed to pay for nearly everything we require or want. Instead of focusing so much on money, however, it would be better to focus on the source of the money (Jesus) and trust Him to provide. Then we can enjoy the perfect love of God that casts out all fear.

Spiritual benefits

Spiritual blessings include the gifts of the Spirit as detailed in 1 Corinthians chapter 12. These gifts are for the benefit of the body of Christ – to build up and edify. The spiritual gifts listed include: *word of wisdom, word of knowledge, faithfulness, gifts of healing, workings of miracles, prophecy, discerning of spirits, speaking in various tongues, and interpretation of tongues.*

In Ephesians 4:11, we further see what are commonly referred to as the five-fold ministry gifts for starting, building up, and shepherding the church of Christ. They are *apostles, prophets, evangelists, pastors, and teachers.*

All of these gifts and appointments within the church are there to benefit each of us in the body of Christ and for expanding the kingdom of God. But as Paul points out in 1 Corinthians chapter 13, the greatest gift is love. 1 Corinthians 13 beautifully describes what perfect love is like; and what it is not like. Love is our greatest aim, and all of the gifts of the Spirit help us propagate and demonstrate that perfect love of God.

Benefits for the righteous recognized by Psalm writers

King David, who began life as a shepherd boy, had a heart after God's own heart according to the Bible. David, as well as other Psalm writers, sums up many of God's blessings in the Psalms. Psalms 68, 103, and 116 contain many.

Psalm 103:1-2 (NKJV – emphasis added)
"Bless the Lord, O my soul; and all that is within me, bless His holy name! Bless the Lord, O my soul and forget not all His benefits:"

God's benefits for the righteous – those who have accepted Christ as their Savior and been spiritually cleansed by the Blood of the Lamb (Christ):
Forgives all our iniquities (sins)
Is a father to orphans and a defender of widows
Delivers those who are bound and brings them into prosperity
Provides for the poor
Leads captivity captive (sets the spiritually captive free to enjoy an abundant life)
Gives us salvation (forgiveness of sins and freedom from illusions and ignorance)
Defeats and frustrates the plans of our enemies
Protects us from accidents and even makes our worst enemies be at peace with us
Heals our diseases
Satisfies us with good things
Crowns us with loving-kindness and tender mercies
Pities those who fear (reverence) Him
Redeems our life from destruction
Satisfies our mouth with good things so our youthfulness is renewed
Executes righteousness
Gives justice to all who are oppressed
Made His ways known to Moses
Is merciful and gracious
Is slow to anger and abounding in mercy
Will not always strive with us or remain angry with us
Has not punished us as we deserve
Has great mercy toward those who fear (reverence) Him
Realizes we are weak, so He is merciful toward us
Remembers that our lives are short – here today and gone tomorrow – but His mercy lasts forever toward those who fear (reverence) Him; and He shows His righteousness to the children and grandchildren of those who reverence Him
Is gracious, righteous, and merciful
Preserves the simple (non-pretentious)

Deals bountifully with those who call on Him and trust Him to deliver them
Provides rest for our soul
Delivers our soul from death, our eyes from tears, and our feet from falling

That is just a small sampling of blessings associated with living a God-focused life with a thankful and grateful heart. Those in themselves seem like more than enough reason to turn your life over to Christ. And remember, God's blessings are not available to the world at large. Blessings showered on the righteous may overflow into the world to bless others, but unbelievers enjoying the overflow will never experience the joy, prosperity, peace, and contentment that come from knowing God. As I said earlier, since God has blessed everyone with certain talents and abilities, we can work in the worldly system to amass money and possessions, but there will be anxiety, stress, and numerous other negative attributes associated with that type of worldly success. With God, you get the blessings without the torment or sorrow.

God's love is enduring and unconditional, but His promises and rewards are conditional on our response. Many Christians I have known go through life living worldly lives which are seemingly no different than non-believers, except they have the knowledge that Christ died for their sins. For that reason, they still live lives filled with partying, drinking, anxiety, fear, discontent, discouragement, and all the other consequences of living unholy because they have the knowledge that Christ died to pay their sin debt, but they have not committed to living a God-centered holy life.

As I have studied God's Word, I have discovered **if** statements always accompany God's promises. God the Father, and Jesus as He walked the earth, "always" said in essence, *"I will do this, if you do that."* Nowhere in the Bible does it say that God accepts or overlooks sin. His rewards have always been conditional – rewards of blessing for obedience in seeking God and obeying Him, or rewards of curses for disobedience and rebellion. I know of no exceptions.

Christ freely surrendered His life and shed His blood on the cross to give us the benefit of a reconciled relationship with the God the Father, but that reconciliation is not automatically conferred to anyone either. **If** we accept that sacrifice by acknowledging with our mouth (confessing) our need for God and asking Christ to come into our hearts – cleansing us and perfecting us into the persons He created us to be – then God the Father sees us through the Blood of Christ – perfect. Until we do that, we are just God's creation and only fit for condemnation and eternal death. It is only through a reconciled relationship paid for by Jesus the Christ that we become acceptable in God's eyes and eligible for His good rewards.

Even after that initial act of salvation and baptism in the name of Jesus the Christ for our remission of sins, Jesus said we must obey Him to prove our love for Him. Old and New Testament alike point to the loving-kindness and mercy of God but also clearly say He requires us to do justly, love others, and obey Him if we want His blessings. If you are acting ugly and refuse to repent of worldly behavior, you will not experience Godly peace and contentment, and you will forfeit many of the blessings reserved for the righteous.

Understanding righteousness

Righteousness basically means knowing and doing right, which only God can do completely. That is why Christ came – to satisfy God the Father's requirements. Only a perfect sacrifice could satisfy God's wrath toward the rebellious human race. The Bible says only blood sacrifice can forgive sins, so it was necessary for Christ to shed His innocent Blood to satisfy God's anger toward humanity and provide for us the opportunity to once again be in a reconciled relationship with the Father. It is not any goodness of ours that pleases God – it is our acceptance and acknowledgment of Christ's sacrifice and our daily attempt to live a life pleasing to God out of thankful and grateful hearts. You will never gain God's approval for your acts of goodness because you will never be perfect, and God demands perfection. But your acts of goodness do earn you rewards. God sees you as perfect and acceptable only when filtered through the Blood of His Lamb – the Christ.

Through pride, many Christians are still trying to earn their salvation through their relative goodness compared to others. Salvation is God's free gift to us – we accept it or we reject it, but we cannot earn it. Blessings are rewards for living an obedient life evidenced through loving God and neighbor. I suspect we will meet self-righteous Christians in heaven who never advanced past the infant stage of their spiritual development, but through ignorance, Satan's deceptions, or pride, they will have forfeited many physical, spiritual, and financial blessings while they walked this earth. Jesus died not only to give us the opportunity for eternal life, but also to give us an abundant life now while we live on this earth.

Concerning salvation, the Bible tells us to work out our salvation with fear and trembling. In other words, don't take your salvation lightly. God the Father sacrificed His only begotten Son for our sake because He loves us that much. If we treat that sacrifice lightly, we can't expect God to bless us with an abundance of peace, contentment, and wealth. Inner peace and contentment only come through a fervent walk with Jesus – trusting in His mercy, being forever thankful and grateful for His acts of mercy and grace and for the blessings He continually gives us to enjoy and share in this earthly life.

Looking for REAL men

Men – the world desperately needs REAL Godly men. I pray that you accept the call to rise above your current level of circumstance.

If you have not yet accepted God's offer of salvation, I encourage you to count the cost and review the benefits. Then, open your mouth and verbally acknowledge your need for Him, confess your sinful nature to Him, and ask Jesus to come into your heart and change you into the man He created you to be. Then go on to dedicate your life to serving God and man with a thankful and grateful heart because of what He has done for you. Enjoy an ever increasing joyful, inner peace-filled, contentment, and prosperous life that accompany a closer walk with Jesus.

Challenge

Humble yourself before God and man and watch God bless your life. A prideful spirit will always cause division between people and cause harm. A humble spirit brings healing, comfort, and reconciliation to people. Seek to be a humble man and ask God for wisdom to live your life as He created you to live it. Turn your life and spirit over to the Lord to direct, and be sure to thank Him for all He does for you. If you can do that, you will see Him work mighty deeds in your life as you live in peace and harmony.

God loves a humble spirit and He grants wisdom to those who ask for it. When we humbly seek Him with our whole heart, mind, soul, and strength, He gives us everything we need and gives us the desires of our heart – good desires that He implants as we seek to do His will and please Him. Seek God and experience the abundant life that God offers – abundance of emotional, physical, and spiritual health, abundance of financial health to be an overflowing blessing to others.

May God bless you and look upon you with His great favor on your journey!

Chapter 7

Making the right connections

Connecting to your church home

*W*e are told in the Bible not to forsake assembling together as a body of believers. To remain healthy spiritually and grow in our knowledge and relationship to God and each other, we must be planted in the church He has reserved for us. In that proper church, we will mature spiritually and emotionally and find the perfect place to share our talents, abilities, and calling from God.

I have noticed that churches, just as individuals, have different personalities and focuses. Therefore, we must be in the church that fits our personality or we will find ourselves frustrated, discontent, and non-contributory.

Many Christians and churches become dysfunctional, in my opinion, because too many people choose a church home for all the wrong reasons. It may be the church closest to their home and they feel all churches are pretty much the same. It may be the church they grew up in and don't want to leave their friends and family to go to another church even if they are not comfortable with or growing spiritually in their home church. It may be a church of the denomination the rest of their family belongs to and they fear upsetting the family by switching to a church of another denomination. It may be a church where their children want to go because they have friends there. Those are reasons that just skim the surface of reasons we use to choose a church home.

Your first course of action in making one of the most important decisions in your life is to pray – asking God to direct you to the church He has prepared for you and prepared you for. He will lead you to the right one if you ask. It may take some time because if you are like most people, you will try several churches before settling into one. When you finally hit the one He wants to plant in, it will feel right, you will be fed spiritually, and you will find areas to fit in and contribute.

This may mean changing denominations which may cause a stir and some disapproving comments by parents and relatives. Be prepared to follow God's leading even if it means losing the approval of close loved ones. If you are in the right church, it will become obvious over time as you continue to grow emotionally and spiritually and increasingly contribute to kingdom building.

When you find the church that feels right, make sure their statement of beliefs agree with what the Bible teaches. There are many Christian churches today preaching and living a secularized gospel that is not compatible with God's Word, so become intimately familiar with your Bible so you can differentiate God's truth from the world's misguided ways that have crept into some churches. Even many Christians today believe there are many ways to Heaven, but Jesus said He is the "only" way to Heaven and eternal life. If you believe anything, else you are not a Christian. Many Christians, through associations with friends of various beliefs and disbeliefs, have been deceived into thinking there are many ways to Heaven, but there aren't.

God told the prophet Jeremiah he should be influencing the people (world), not letting the people (world) influence him. I am disappointed and surprised to see how many Christian churches today have been more influenced by the world than them influencing the world. Many Christians, and subsequently Christian churches, have been deceived by Satan to believe the lie and reject the truth about many worldly lusts and practices, and we are seeing the negative consequences played out in the morality of our modern society daily.

I know too many professing Christians who have never read their Bible or truly sought a closer relationship with God, and their lifestyles reflect that reality. We are bombarded with worldly influences throughout our day, so if we do not spend considerable time reading God's Word and seeking Him through prayer and fellowship with other mature Christians, how can we expect to know God's will and conform our nature to God's nature instead of the world's nature? Without diligently seeking God – choosing life and blessing – we will automatically choose the world – death and cursing.

Advantages to your church connection

I have observed that most non-believers tend to socialize with only those who are like them in hobbies or career path. That can lead to a very narrow worldview. The wonderful thing I have noticed with the body of Christ is we have individuals from all walks of life worshipping and working side-by-side. This diversity in talents and abilities avails us to expand our knowledge and make connections with people who can help us in an untold number of ways. Having our salvation, love for Jesus, and love for each other in common, doctors, lawyers, car mechanics, business owners, janitors, teachers, and etcetera share talents and abilities for our common benefit – causing the members of the body to grow spiritually, emotionally, physically, financially, and in many other ways. Christ brings us together for the benefit of the whole and to benefit us individually, promoting the abundant life Christ died to give us.

We also need to hear the Word of God on a regular basis to keep us growing in faith, understanding, and wisdom. Without the connection to other faithful believers on a regular basis and constant reminding of God's love and faithfulness, we can easily stray through the influence of the world around us. We need to stay in tune with God's will to be spiritually healthy, and much of that tuning is done in the church God pleases to put us in. We thrive when we love and serve one another, and the church body God pleases to put us in provides a perfect outlet to do that serving and sharing.

Your future – will you choose the good life?

Christ willingly sacrificed His life so you could enjoy a peace-filled, content, prosperous life now and forevermore. The choice is yours. Living a life focused on loving God and serving (loving) leads to the abundant life Christ promised all who believe and obey.

Since God has blessed you with certain talents and abilities, you can no doubt carve out a life of relative worldly success and accumulate money and things using those God-given talents and abilities. But if you choose to focus on doing it your way, you will find it does not bring the peace, contentment, or satisfaction you think it will. The love of money always brings curses with it. On the contrary, if you focus on seeking the Lord Jesus with all your heart, mind, soul, and strength, you will find yourself increasingly enjoying the peace-filled, content, abundant life that Christ died to give you as you find yourself prospering in everything you set your hand to do. Those are promises from God, and He never breaks His promises.

You must choose – blessing or curse. You can try keeping one foot in Heaven and one foot in the world as many do, but if you do, you will find yourself constantly torn and frustrated because you will not be enjoying the benefits of either walk.

If you choose to put your entire focus on this world and what this temporary world has to offer, you may enjoy your fruits for a season, but disappointment awaits you after each temporary enjoyment you experience.

If you choose to put your entire focus on Heaven and letting the Holy Spirit direct your life in this present temporary world, you will find your inner peace and contentment increase as God satisfies your every need and desire in His perfect timing.

I have observed people walking each of these three paths, but the only one that ever brings lasting peace, contentment, and satisfaction is doing it God's way – loving Him and loving your neighbors as yourself. That is the whole of your duty – loving God as evidenced by obeying His commands and loving others as much as you love yourself – focusing on serving their needs.

Choose the path of blessing. Choose to become a REAL man God's way!

Prologue

*T*he instruction provided in this book will lead you down the path toward the Godly success, peace, and content prosperity that everyone seeks. It is not intended to be a fix-all remedy cookbook with step-by-step instructions to lead you through each step of your life. As with all Christian books, and all of my books, it leads you to the source of your provision and protection – Jesus – with a little more understanding and knowledge than you had before you read it. I have given you the information consistent with God's Word to mature you in your relationships to God and the world around you.

I am confident there are many good materials available to help you in that journey. I have found that as you seek God for wisdom, understanding, and direction, He will lead you to books, music, people, churches, and many other resources to grow you closer to Him. Since you have read this book, I know for a certainty that this was no accident. There is information in this book that God intends for your spiritual development to draw you into a closer relationship with Him so He can prosper and mature you in new ways.

I thank you for sharing your life with me by reading this work from my heart. As with all of my published works, I seek to give you practical wisdom and guidance to lead you to the source of all blessings – God the Father through the Blood of His sinless sacrifice, Jesus the Christ, and the Holy Spirit of truth that proceeds from the Father to every believer who obeys His Word and seeks Him with their whole heart, mind, soul, and strength. Be one of those believers. Seek God continually and see Him work in your life.

God Bless!

Recommended reading from Dennis G. Aaberg

Topic Bible Studies Addressing Everyday Problems and Questions – Series 1
   ISBN 1591603986
   Suggested retail price: $16.99

Topic Bible Studies Addressing Everyday Problems and Questions – Series 2
   ISBN 9781615792092
   Suggested retail price: $16.99

Topic Bible Studies Addressing Everyday Problems and Questions provide thought-provoking, self-searching Bible Studies designed to bring you joy, peace, and contentment as you grow to see the Lord Jesus as a faithful and trusted friend. The studies purpose to mature your faith to where you can live a stress-free content life with the inner peace that only God's Holy Spirit can provide.

Seducing Spirits – The Battle for Your Soul
   ISBN 978-1-60266-622-1 (hardcopy)
   Suggested retail price: $22.99
   ISBN 978-1-60266-621-4 (paperback)
   Suggested retail price: $14.99

Most Christians with some level of background in the Scriptures agree that we are involved in spiritual warfare and that in the end times, that battle will intensify. That belief, however, is often a general acknowledgement that Satan is alive and trying to deceive the Saints.

Now, in *Seducing Spirits: the Battle for Your Soul*, Dennis Aaberg provides a significant service to the Church by systematically and comprehensively presenting the nature of the spiritual battle we are all called to wage. The various spirits, or demons, that affect a whole range of sinful behavior are identified; the nature of the battle taking place in the heavenly realm is clarified; and the reassuring provision of the

Armor of God for our protection is examined. Then, Dennis outlines twenty-seven disciplines that will help you live free in Christ – giving both young and old helpful guidelines that will enable them to resist the seducing spirits of the age.

As with all Minister Aaberg's writings, the entire work is extremely practical, the substance of his thesis is thoroughly biblical, and the abundance of Scriptural quotations leaves you with a sense of, "Thus saith the Lord!"

Seducing Spirits will sharpen your spiritual perceptions and give you an advantage in victoriously walking with Christ, even in these challenging last days.

Pastor Timothy A. Johnson
Executive Director, Minnesota Church Ministries Association
Bishop/Executive Director, Minnesota Church Ministries Association – Africa

Jesus' Last Seminar – Preaching Love and Unity
ISBN 9781615792436
Suggested retail price: $10.99

Jesus' Last Seminar provides a clear understanding of God's triune nature, Jesus' mandate for believers to walk in love and unity, and a warning to those within His body who produce no fruit.

Knowing His time on earth was short, Jesus crammed much of Christian theology into a few last words with His disciples in the upper room before His betrayal in the Garden of Gethsemane. Discover the essential teachings of Jesus in Jesus' Last Seminar, and then apply them to your life so that you can experience the peace of heart and mind that God wills for you.

For more information and other offerings by Dennis Aaberg see Aaberg Ministries' website.

Email: aabergministries@earthlink.net
Website: www.aabergministries.com